Praise for *The Comic He*
Serious Story Structure for Fal

"1. Stop writing your comedy script.
2. Read this book.
3. Start writing again with the knowledge you need."
—**Tim Ferguson**, comedian, film director, screenwriter, and author of *The Cheeky Monkey: Writing Narrative Comedy*

"In *The Comic Hero's Journey*, Steve Kaplan stands the classic, dramatic hero's journey on its head and shakes out a set of guidelines for the unique journey of the comic hero. With examples from popular comedies, he shows how the assumptions and starting points of comic heroes are subtly different from those of conventional dramatic heroes, and he gives clear principles that will help you tell comedy stories that are funny but also emotionally engaging. If you want to crack the code of comedy, here is the nutcracker!"
—**Chris Vogler**, author, *The Writer's Journey*

"Steve Kaplan's book is nothing short of brilliant. With an abundance of examples from film and television, and Steve's clear (and funny) insights, *The Comic Hero's Journey* is an absolutely essential guide for anyone wanting to create comedy that doesn't just make us laugh, but reveals our flawed and heroic humanity."
—**Michael Hauge**, world-renowned story expert, script consultant, and bestselling author of *Writing Screenplays That Sell* and *Storytelling Made Easy*

"Comedy king and guru Steve Kaplan rubbed together all the comedy pointers you'd ever want to know, creating fire with comedy flint, and wrote a guide sure to help you succeed if you take the craft of writing funny seriously. Make sure this book is on your shelf!"
—**Devo Cutler-Rubenstein**, former studio executive; author of *Dating Your Character . . . A Sexy Guide to Screenwriting*; executive producer / cowriter of award-winning comedy documentary *Not Afraid to Laugh*

"I absolutely loved it! I found it illuminating and full of both laughs and wisdom—what a great combination! For any writer trying to craft a great screenplay, information and inspiration are the names of the game. You have to read books. Watch movies. Check out other scripts. Well, Steve's new book *The Comic Hero's Journey* delivers on both the information and inspiration fronts, and also does something just as difficult: entertains. I came to the book for the knowledge. I stayed for the laughs. This is invaluable, insightful stuff for anyone—writer, director, producer, or executive—who takes their comedy seriously."
—**Lee Jessup**, screenwriting coach; author, *Getting It Write: An Insider's Guide to a Screenwriting Career*

"*The Comic Hero's Journey* is a delightful and insightful page-turner, not only for those who wish to write better film or TV comedies, but for anyone wanting to "get" more clearly what makes film comedy work!"
—**Andrew Horton**, Jeanne H. Smith Professor of Film & Media Studies, Emeritus, University of Oklahoma

"If Shakespeare had a jester, Kaplan was his name."
—**Dov S-S Simens**, dean, Hollywood Film Institute

"Informative and inspiring, *The Comic Hero's Journey* is a valuable addition to any writer's library and a must-have for anyone daring to take on the challenge of writing really good comedy. Insightful and encouraging."
—**Pamela Jaye Smith**, mythologist and MYTHWORKS founder, international speaker-consultant, award-winning writer, producer, director, and author, *Beyond the Hero's Journey*

"What separates drama and comedy when it comes to the 'hero's journey'? Steve Kaplan sheds a brilliant light on the comedic hero and how to approach crafting the comedy screenplay. If you want to write a script that can't be ignored, I highly recommend you read this book."
—**Jen Grisanti**, story / career consultant; writing instructor for NBC; author

"Writing comedy is a serious journey. It can also be intimidating and scary. Following the concepts and structures delineated in this book will make your journey so much easier. Steve Kaplan explains why comedies don't usually fit into traditional dramatic narrative structures, and he identifies new beats, which are very useful to the comedy writer. Really useful, practical examples illustrate a fresh take on comic structure. You end up laughing as much as you do learning! If you're looking for inspiration and support to write your next comedy script, you'll review great comedic scenes from movies to get you inspired, and useful character archetypes and structure to get your script moving."
—**Matthew Kalil**, story consultant; author, *The Three Wells of Screenwriting*

"There are lots of books on structuring a screenplay, but none that are specific to comedy. This invaluable step-by-step approach to that daunting task takes the mystery out of the writing process and gives you the specific information you need to write a successful comedy script. Not only is the system Kaplan suggests an original approach to the process, it's easy to follow, and makes for an entertaining read."
—**Carole Kirschner**, author, *Hollywood Game Plan*

"Steve Kaplan brilliantly applies the principles of classic mythic story structure and character archetypes to the comedy genre. An eye-opening look at how the same tools that helped create dramatic classics like *Star Wars* can, with a bit of an interpretive twist, be utilized to craft compelling comedic narratives."
—**Diane Drake**, screenwriter, *Only You, What Women Want*

The Comic
HERO'S
JOURNEY

SERIOUS STORY STRUCTURE
FOR FABULOUSLY FUNNY FILMS

STEVE KAPLAN

MICHAEL WIESE PRODUCTIONS

For Kathrin
Otherwise, the past forty years have been a terrible mistake

Published by Michael Wiese Productions
12400 Ventura Blvd. #1111
Studio City, CA 91604
(818) 379-8799, (818) 986-3408 (FAX)
mw@mwp.com
www.mwp.com

Cover design by Johnny Ink. www.johnnyink.com
Interior design by William Morosi
Copyediting by Ross Plotkin
Printed by McNaughton & Gunn

Manufactured in the United States of America

Table of Contents

Acknowledgments

The author gratefully acknowledges the invaluable help, again, of my wife Kathrin King Segal and my friend, Rhonda Hayter, both of whom contributed notes, advice, perspective, and corrections on every page and every chapter, and saved me countless times from myself—grammar-wise, spelling-wise, and all-other-ways-wise. Any errors that remain are mine, and mine alone.

I'm also indebted to my friend, comedy scholar Professor Andrew Horton, who read early chapters and provided critical guidance; to Chris Vogler, whose book I love, whose friendship I cherish and who took it in good stride when I told him I was pirating his title for this book; and to publisher and friend, Ken Lee, for counsel and advice and the ever-present boot in the rear, all of which I'm grateful for.

Finally, I'm grateful to all the artists, writers, directors, performers, and producers who have created the films mentioned in this book. You've given us the gift of laughter, and as Preston Sturges wrote in *Sullivan's Travels*: "There's a lot to be said for making people laugh. Did you know that that's all some people have? It isn't much, but it's better than nothing in this cockeyed caravan."

1.

The Schlemiel with a Thousand Faces

"Eagles may soar, but weasels don't get sucked into jet engines."

—Steven Wright

In the beginning was the film, and the film was *Star Wars*.

OK, that's not how that book goes, but it's not a bad way to start off this one.

This book owes a big debt of gratitude to Joseph Campbell and his *Hero With a Thousand Faces*, and an even bigger debt to my friend Chris Vogler, whose study of Campbell led to *The Writer's Journey*, his insightful melding of Campbell's mono-myth with screenplay structure and storytelling.

If you've never heard of it before, or just to refresh your memory, The Hero's Journey consists of:

1. Ordinary World
2. Call to Adventure
3. Refusal of the Call
4. Meeting With the Mentor

If you think about *Star Wars*, it closely tracks the steps in Campbell's Hero's Journey. Near the beginning of the film, we meet our Hero, farm boy Luke, living in the boring old desert world of Tatooine (**Ordinary World**) when he stumbles across the holographic message from Princess Leia (**Call to Adventure**). Following the message he meets with Obi-Wan Kenobi (**Meeting with the Mentor**) but refuses to go to Alderaan with him (**Refusal of the Call**) because he "has so much work to do" and because "it's all so far away."

He returns home, however, only to find that his aunt and uncle have been murdered by the Empire's Stormtroopers, and returns to Obi-wan declaring that he now wants to go to Alderaan, "I want to learn the ways of the Force and become a Jedi like my father!"

Traveling to the seedy port town of Mos Eisley (**Crossing the First Threshold**), Obi-Wan enlists the help of rogue smugglers Han Solo and Chewbacca of the Millennium Falcon, where Luke practices wielding the Force (**Tests, Allies, and Enemies**). Jumping through hyperspace to what they think is Alderaan, they discover it's been destroyed and are pulled aboard the Death Star (**Approach to the Inmost Cave**), where in rescuing Princess Leia, they must fight off the Stormtroopers and Darth Vader, only to face death in the trash compactor and then witness the death of Luke's mentor Obi-Wan (**Ordeal**).

At the rebel base, Luke realizes his wish: he gets to be a fighter pilot for the Rebellion. Plus, he gets a kiss on the cheek from Princess Leia! (**Reward—Seizing the Sword**) Luke and the fleet return to attack the Death Star (**The Road Back**), where he faces almost certain death. As Darth Vader zeros in on Luke's starfighter, Luke hears and heeds the voice of Obi-Wan and becomes one with the Force as Han Solo returns just in the nick of time (**Resurrection**), destroying the Death Star! With that stunning victory, Luke, Han, and Chewy mount the platform where Princess Leia honors them for saving the Rebellion and restoring hope to the galaxy. Luke is now a man in full (**Return With the Elixir**).

But you knew all that already.

So, what happens in a comedy? A comic hero or heroine also goes on a journey. In some aspects, it's very similar to what Chris Vogler and Joseph Campbell write about in their books. But in many ways, it's quite, quite different.

When Luke's family is killed, he bravely and solemnly vows to "learn the ways of the Force and become a Jedi like my father." A comic hero would have un-bravely tried to run away so as to not get killed. Throughout *Star Wars*, Luke is adventurous, brave, and stalwart. When he's chasing after R2D2 and there's the threat that the Sand People might be about, he grabs a rifle, and with no small amount of pluck tells C3PO, "Let's take a look!"

Comic Heroes tend to be pluck-deficient. Vogler writes that "heroes show us how to deal with death," but comic heroes show us how to deal with life. "Heroes," according to Vogler, "accept the possibility of sacrifice," but comic heroes have to be dragged kicking and screaming, and even then, they try to run away from it.

In *The Wizard of Oz*, as Dorothy's three companions plan to storm the Wicked Witch's castle the Cowardly Lion says to Tin Man and Scarecrow outside the Wicked Witch's castle:

```
         COWARDLY LION
All right, I'll go in there for
Dorothy. Wicked Witch or no Wicked
Witch, guards or no guards, I'll tear
them apart. I may not come out alive,
but I'm going in there. There's only
one thing I want you fellows to do.

      TIN WOODSMAN, SCARECROW
What's that?

         COWARDLY LION
Talk me out of it!
```

The hero decides to go on the adventure. The comic hero often has no choice.

The hero usually has a wise old man; the comic hero often meets an idiot who inadvertently says something that can teach him a thing or two.

For many years (and in many places) I have taught workshops on the Hidden Tools of Comedy, and often my students have asked me about story structure. And the more I've thought about it, the more I've come to realize that there is a very particular kind of story structure in comedy.

There have been a lot of books written about story structure in feature films. I should know; many of them are written by friends of mine. But there have been few that deal directly and explicitly with story structure in comedies. Pablo Picasso reportedly once said that, "Good artists create; great artists steal." So that's what I did—I decided to steal (only please replace the horrid word *steal* with the more stately term, *pay homage to*) Chris's title, and write my own book about story structure, but specifically as it shows up in comedic features.

THE COMIC HERO'S JOURNEY

In the Comic Hero's Journey, your protagonist goes through a trans-formative experience as well. The steps of that are:

1. The Normal World

In the normal world, your protagonists are damaged, broken peo-ple living in a damaged, broken world. Only they don't know it. They think they're fine, they think life is perfect, that their world is working fine, until . . .

2. WTF?

. . . the shit hits the fan, the apple cart is overturned, all hell breaks loose—boy wakes up to find he's a thirty-year-old man, guy finds that every day is still Groundhog Day—and when it does, there's a desperate attempt to return to the Normal World in . . .

3. Reactions

This is where your protagonist at first desperately tries to put his normal world back together. In *Big*, this is Tom Hanks tak-ing a bike and riding out to where the fairground was, and then coming back home and telling his mom, "Mom, I wished on a fortune-telling machine and I got big!" But no one believes him, which leads to . . .

4. Connections

In the Comic Hero's Journey, your character starts to make con-nections that they have never made before. Love interests, allies, unexpected friends. And because of those connections they go off in . . .

5. New Directions

They go off on paths they hadn't thought about going off on before, leading to the Discovered Goals. But just when all seems well there's the inevitable . . .

6. Disconnection

. . . when they break up, and it looks like all is lost. In *Dodgeball*, this was when Vince Vaughn seemingly throws the game and sells out his team. But just then there's a revitalization and recommit-ment to achieving the discovered goal and there's the . . .

7.   Race to the Finish

In romantic comedy, that's a race to the altar. That's Dustin Hoffman racing to the church, or Billy Crystal running through Manhattan to try to get to the love of his life before it's too late. There's always some hectic action in which the hero, the protagonist, and usually the protagonist's friends and allies, desperately try to achieve the final goal. In *The 40-Year-Old Virgin*, Steve Carell realizes that no he doesn't want to go to bed with the bookstore girl (who's in the bathtub pleasuring herself—you had to be there) and realizes that he really loves Catherine Keener, so he has to race to go get her. And of course, since he doesn't drive a car, it's a race to an almost disastrous finish on a bicycle.

After the race to the finish there's the denouement or tag or even just a beat, which gives us the sense that there's a better world ahead.

So, let's get started . . .

* * *

Except, first, let me give you a caveat. This is not a formula. It's not a template. All these steps happen in most well-structured comedies, but not necessarily in this order. Most people think of the low point in a comedy as occurring about three-quarters of the way through the film. And it does, in most films. But not in all. In *Groundhog Day*, Bill Murray tries to kill himself about halfway through the movie. In *Tropic Thunder*, the platoon breaks up and Ben Stiller tries to go it alone again about halfway through. Other movies may skip or skimp on one step or another. In most movies, all of these elements are somewhere in the movie, but do they HAVE to be in this order? No.

There are a lot of great, idiosyncratic, atypical movies. And while most comedies begin in the Normal World and end with Race to the Finish, yours doesn't need to. Your comic hero is on his or her own journey. The routes may be similar in many ways, but as they often say in the showroom, your mileage may vary.

So, as Philip Roth once wrote, "So. Now vee may perhaps to begin. Yes?"

2.

A Guy Walks Into a Bar

THE NORMAL WORLD

"Two wrongs are only the beginning."
—STEVEN WRIGHT

LET'S START WITH THE NORMAL WORLD.

In the beginning of the Hero's Journey, our heroes are exceptional. Joseph Campbell writes that the adventure was not one of "discovery but rediscovery. The godly powers sought and dangerously won are revealed to have been within the heart of the hero all the time." He (or she) has hidden greatness within, but at the start, our heroes are unaware of their undiscovered virtues. They are, as Chris Vogler puts it, "ready to enter the world of adventure."

However, in the Comic Hero's Journey, your protagonist, the comic hero, does not have greatness within. Your protagonist is as far from greatness within as is humanly possible, and sometimes, even more than that. He wants a "world of adventure" like he wants a hole in the head. Your protagonist is usually a dweeb or a jerk or some other kind of a misbegotten misanthrope. In *Big* he's bullied and not big enough to go on a ride with the girl of his dreams. In *Groundhog Day*, Bill Murray is an egotistical a-hole. In *Bridesmaids*, Kristen Wiig's low self-esteem has her sleeping with a guy she *knows* doesn't like her. In the Normal World, **the comic hero's initial state is flawed** in some vital way; there's a hole inside them; their way of being in the world is deeply, deeply flawed. As Ricky Gervais has said, "No one wants to see handsome, clever people do brilliant things brilliantly. Who wants to see that? You want to see a putz having a go. And failing. And coming through at the end."

At the beginning of the Normal World, the comic hero's life does not work, ***only they don't know it!*** They think they're fine, and their world is perfect. To them, it's the normal state of affairs and for the most part they've accepted it. If you have a protagonist who comes out in the first act and says, "You know, I . . . I'm just not doing what I should do in life. I'm, I'm, I'm unhappy," you've written a drama. Because the more aware your characters are of their own state of being, the more dramatic those moments are. One of the tools in *The Hidden Tools of Comedy* is the idea of the **Non-Hero**. A Non-Hero lacks skills. Rather than constructing a comic character by making them the most ridiculous excuse for a person you've ever met (I'm looking at you, Deuce Bigalow), a Non-Hero is simply someone who lacks some, if not all, of the essential skills and tools with which to accomplish their utmost goals, or just get through the day. One of the most basic skills is awareness. Heroes have it; Non-Heroes, for the most part, don't.

One of the most important skills that the Non-Hero lacks is knowing, because a non-hero doesn't know. Not that they're stupid, but they **don't know**. They don't have information. The more information you give your characters, the more dramatic they become, the more heroic they become. If a character is having a hard time, and they're aware that they're having a hard time and they're agonizing over it, that's drama. In comedies, characters are blissfully unaware. They're blindly going into situations. And we in the audience can see what's going on, but they don't.

Rather than the inchoate unhappiness of a dramatic hero before he finds his quest, the comic hero is blithely unaware of what we in the audience can see is a stacked deck against them, a flawed existence, a screwed-up way of living.

In *Groundhog Day*, Bill Murray thinks that all he needs is to go to a bigger TV station in a bigger market, but we can see that he's really a cynical, stunted soul, and that his way of being in the world isn't successful.

In *Stranger Than Fiction*, Will Ferrell plays an IRS agent who lacks flexibility, spontaneity, and is a total stick in the mud.

In *Tootsie*, Dustin Hoffman is a great acting teacher, and maybe even a great actor, but who knows? No one will hire him because he's such an asshole. When he barges into his agent's office, he's unaware that his lack of professional success might have anything to do with himself.

In *(500) Days of Summer*, Joseph Gordon-Levitt is going through the motions writing bad greeting cards; in *Bridesmaids*, Kristen Wiig's a mess with a string of failed relationships behind her; in *40-Year-Old Virgin*, he's, uh . . . well, uh . . . dammit, he's 40 years old and he's a virgin!

In the Comic Hero's Journey, that's the protagonist's normal state. And the normal state is fucked.

TRANSFORMATION

All comedy is transformational. The whole point of the Normal World is to set up your protagonist for that eventual change. You might think that all you need to do is put your nice, normal hero in a crazy, fucked-up situation and see how it all shakes out. Well, don't.

Take *Groundhog Day*, which I mention a lot because it's one of my favorite films.[1] Well, in the initial draft of *Groundhog Day* that Danny Rubin wrote, Phil Connors is just a nice guy that shit happens to. After page 70, he and Rita try to figure it out. It's seventy pages of him just

---

[1] In case you've never seen it, you can read a summary at en.wikipedia.org/wiki/Groundhog_Day_(film). But really, you should just go watch it.

getting his ass kicked for no goddamn good reason. Don't pull wings off of a fly just because you can. There needs to be a reason that you, the deity in this universe, have decided Job needs to suffer. You're making Job suffer. Why? If he's already perfect, why are you torturing this person? In the Comic Hero's Journey, our protagonists need it. Kristen Wiig needs to get shaken out of her rut in *Bridesmaids*. Phil Connors needs to be a better person in *Groundhog Day*. And what a terrific deity Phil has, who will pluck him out of space and time just so he can be a better person. That's some cool deity.

INITIAL GOAL

Another big difference between the classic Joseph Campbell hero and the Comic Hero is that the classic hero often has a major overall goal that he or she tries to accomplish throughout the course of the story. In the Hero's Journey, the hero usually has a goal in the beginning and they either achieve it—happiness. Or they don't achieve it—tragedy. But it's the same goal. In the beginning Luke wants to join the rebellion; guess what? He joins the rebellion. He saves the rebellion. Often, the initial goal is the end goal.

In comedy, that's not true. Many of your protagonist's goals in the beginning of a comedy are outer goals. These **initial goals**[2] are usually selfish and shortsighted and certainly are not addressing their inner needs. (These initial goals will eventually be replaced by **discovered goals** as the characters transform during the course of the narrative.)

Sandra Bullock just wants to lead a quiet life in *While You Were Sleeping*. Will Ferrell in *Stranger Than Fiction* just wants to do his audits and be left alone.

In *Shrek*, what does Shrek want? All he wants is to get the multitude of fairy tale characters out of his swamp and be left alone like he

---

[2] Goals are specific to feature films, because goals have specific, defined ends—they're either achieved or not achieved. But in sitcoms, it would be wrong to assign your main characters goals. (You don't want the sitcom to end, you want to go into syndication!) My friend Ellen Sandler, a genius and the author of *The TV Writer's Workbook*, calls it the character's **driving force**. It's not a goal they can achieve, it's the force that wakes them up and gets them out of bed every day. This driving force hopefully will propel them into and through at least 100 episodes. (Voila! Syndication!)

always has been. He wants to get his world back to the way it was—his Normal World.

In the apocalyptic comedy *This Is the End*, the goal is for Seth Rogen and his buddies to just ride out the last days without necessarily having to change their hedonistic behavior at all. In *Spy*, Melissa McCarthy is an intelligence support analyst who only wants the dashing spy played by Jude Law to fall in love with her.

In *40-Year-Old Virgin*, Steve Carell's goal is simply to wake up, go to work, come back alone, make an omelet alone, play his video games. To him, that's the length and breadth of his world. That's what he's comfortable with, and that's how he's going to stay. In *Tropic Thunder*, Robert Downey Jr. and Ben Stiller just want to make this terrible Vietnam-era movie. To the Comic Hero, life is fine, and it would be perfect if only . . .

FLAWED OR ABSENT RELATIONSHIPS

In the Normal World, there are **flawed or absent relationships**. If you're going to write a screenplay about someone who's a worm that's about to turn, it's best if you don't start them in a happy, monogamous relationship where everything's going well. If you're trying to build a protagonist who's kind of a loser, having a supportive girlfriend or boyfriend undercuts their ineptitude. Your hero is living in Mom's basement, playing Dungeons and Dragons by himself. A girlfriend? Are you kidding me? If someone's cool enough to have a girlfriend or a boyfriend, maybe they're not as flawed as they need to be. Even if he's a great guy, like in *Sleepless in Seattle*, make sure relationships are absent or flawed. In *Sleepless*, his wife is dead. He doesn't have or want to pursue another relationship. In fact, it's ruining his life, and his son is motivated to get on the phone to call in a radio station to get him another wife.

Relationships flawed or absent: In *Forgetting Sarah Marshall*, Jason Segal's cool girlfriend (Kristen Bell) dumps him right at the start. In *Groundhog Day*, Bill Murray is kind of a misanthrope, and all his relationships are superficial. In *Bridesmaids*, Kristen Wiig's hook-up is an obnoxious Jon Hamm, who won't even let her sleep over. Steve Carell in *The 40-Year-Old Virgin* has no real relationships except for the elderly couple with whom he shares viewing episodes of *Survivor*. He doesn't have any close friends, certainly no female relationships.

In *This Is the End*, we can see that the relationship between Seth Rogen and Jay Baruchel is deeply flawed. Both are enjoying a moderate bit of show-business success, especially Seth, who thinks that as long as he can party hardy and do more drugs and hang out with James Franco, his life is okay. Jay, though, expresses disdain for Los Angeles, yet is unaware of his envy and his desire to achieve the same show-business success that his peers are attaining. On one hand, he doesn't want to be like overly privileged young movie stars such as Seth and James Franco, but he's also jealous of them. Neither Seth nor Jay are in good places, but the more self-aware Jay is not really doing anything to repair his relationships.

SEEDS

The Normal World can last anywhere from five to twenty-five minutes, setting up your protagonist's Normal World before the **WTF**, the big event, the catalyst that's going to send everything spinning out of orbit.

During this time, you want to plant **the seeds of conflict and resolution** and set up the conventions for the story. In an interview with Michel Hazanavicius, the writer-director of *The Artist*, he states that, "You have fifteen minutes to tell the audience, 'These are the rules.' *Jurassic Park* teaches us to expect a T. rex, but if a T. rex comes thirty minutes into *When Harry Met Sally*, you won't believe it. So [in *The Artist*] we start with the right opening credits, all together on the page, and the narrative cards with the right font, Silentina, and then everything follows." Hazanavicius calls this the "grammar of the movie," and like grammar in writing, it's not the content itself—but without it, the content collapses.

Almost everything that's going to be developed in the screenplay needs to be dropped into the Normal World. A tenet of screenwriting is that if you have Act 3 problems, they're really Act 1 problems. I agree with that, except for the fact that every Act 2 problem is *also* an Act 1 problem. If you're stuck or bolloxed up in Acts 2 or 3, it's because you haven't properly prepared things in Act 1.

Everything that you want to happen, everything that you want to pay off should be seeded, if possible, in the Normal World. A great example of this is the opening of *Back to the Future*. Everything that comes to pass and pays off in Acts Two and Three in this brilliantly constructed film is set up in those first five to ten pages—his dweeby family, the audition that doesn't go well, skateboarding. In fact, a lot of it happens during the credits, as the camera pans across Doc Brown's office and laboratory and you see all the pictures and articles of things that are going to come into play later on. The camera doesn't stop and say, "Now, pay attention to this: thirty years ago, this happened." But it's there. Part of the delight of the Robert Zemeckis movie is seeing seeds come to fruition that were sown in the first act, in the first ten minutes, or in some cases, in the first minute and a half.

Do not bring in a neighbor whom we've never met or seen before on page 82 to start to resolve things. That's a Deus ex Machina, the God in the Machine. The Ancient Greeks used to end tragedies by lowering an actor playing one of the gods down to the stage to settle all the matters that had been bedeviling the other characters for the first four acts. If you want to have a lightning bolt send your hero back to the future in Act 3, you need to mention in Act 1 that the clock in the town square was struck by lightning. Any crazy idea is great, as long as it's set up. We need to see how ideas are planted and germinated to appreciate them when they bloom.

Sometimes it's not feasible to plant everything in the first ten or twenty minutes of the movie. An example of this is in *Tootsie*, where the climactic live broadcast near the end of the film is set up by introducing the idea of "mistakes, retakes, and live broadcasts" in Act 2. In this case, the protagonist doesn't enter the world of the soap opera until after the Normal World, but the point is to seed that information *as soon as it's possible*.

MASK TO MENSCH

One of the seeds you'll plant in Act 1 is what we call **Mask to Mensch**. Your protagonist starts off wearing a mask, a façade that hides, from himself as well as us, the good man or woman he or she will eventually become—a *mensch*.[3] Your characters are pretending, most successfully to themselves, unaware of the possibility that there's a better person inside. Along the way the mask is dropped and the good person, the *mensch*, emerges. Sometime during the Normal World, you want to make sure that the audience glimpses, no matter how fleetingly, the *mensch* behind the mask, a hint of the person they might become. In the Normal World, we mostly see the false front. When the mask is momentarily removed to reveal the *mensch*, remember that your protagonist is unaware of it.

In the beginning of *Groundhog Day*, you don't see Bill Murray having a moment where he goes, *You know, maybe if I was a better person . . . maybe better things would happen.* No. But he does have a moment early on when he's looking at Rita for the first time. The station manager is telling him he has to go to Punxsutawney, but he can take Rita with him. "She'll be fun," he says. And Bill Murray sees her for the first time, and the camera pushes in and lingers on him just looking at her. Without a quip. Without a cynical aside. In that moment, he's no longer a jerk or an asshole. He's just a guy looking at a girl.

---

[3] This concept is similar to what Michael Hauge talks about in his DVD *The Hero's Two Journeys*, in which he talks about identity and essence. But here it's in Yiddish, so it's entirely different.

. . . And then it's gone. He says, "Yeah, she's fun . . . but not my kind of fun." He snaps right back to being a jerk. But for a moment, you've given the audience a glimpse of who he may become and why they should like and root for this character.

Another example is in *(500) Days of Summer*. In one of Tom's (Joseph Gordon-Levitt) first conversation with Summer (Zooey Deschanel)—on Day 8, actually—she asks him how long he's been working at the greeting card company.

>   SUMMER
>   So have you worked here long?
>
>   TOM
>   About three . . . or four years.
>
>   SUMMER
>   Wow. You always wanted to write
>   greeting cards?
>
>   TOM
>   Nah, don't even want to do it now.
>
>   SUMMER
>   Well, you should do something else,
>   then.
>
>   TOM
>   Yeah, I studied to be an architect
>   actually.
>
>   SUMMER
>   You did? That's cool. What happened
>   there?
>
>   TOM
>   Didn't work out. Eh, I needed a job
>   and, here we are.
>
>   SUMMER
>   Were you any good?

                    TOM
            (hands her a card)
Well I wrote this one.

                    SUMMER
            (reading)
"Today You're a Man. Mazel Tov on
your Bar Mitzvah."

                    TOM
It's a big seller.

                    SUMMER
I meant as an architect?

                    TOM
I doubt it.

                    SUMMER
Well, I'd say you're a perfectly
... adequate... greeting card
writer.

She walks back to her cubicle at the
other end of the hall.

Tom watches her walk away, completely
enamored.

He sits down at his desk and sets out to
work. But before he does, his eyes fall
on a sketch he drew of a house. It's
dated 2001 and it's the only architecture
sketch on his wall

Glancing across the office at Summer, Tom is inspired to begin
drawing an architectural sketch of a building, but then quickly, giving
into his internal doubts and sense of inadequacy, partially erases it,
crumples it and tosses it away. For a moment, an all-too-brief moment,
we get a sense of the man who Tom could become, before he slips on
his mask of millennial "couldn't give a fuck."

INITIAL LOSS

Like Tom's lost dreams of being an architect, many comedies start with, or right after, a painful **initial loss**. Kristen Wiig's bakery shop has been lost to the economic downturn at the beginning of *Bridesmaids*. Tim Allen is a washed-up TV star whose sci-fi show was cancelled years ago and whose castmates hate him in *Galaxy Quest*. Riley has lost her childhood home and all her friends in *Inside Out*. Disney and Pixar's body count include Bambi and Nemo's mother, and Simba and Cinderella's dad. These losses add dimension and weight to the character, and overcoming these losses adds stature and importance to our Heroes eventual transformation and (hopefully) triumph.

THEME IMPLIED

In the Normal World, your **theme is introduced**, and implied or hinted at through the dialogue, without putting your thumb too heavily on the scales. (In Chapter Four we'll talk a little more about theme and how it relates to premise, the development of the premise, and how it's intertwined in the structure.)

For instance, in *Groundhog Day* as they're driving up to Punxsutawney, Chris Elliott turns to Bill Murray and says, "What do you have against the groundhog? I covered the swallows going back to Capistrano four years in a row." And Bill Murray says, very offhandedly, "Somebody's going to see me interviewing a groundhog and think I don't have a future." Which is, in fact, what's going to happen. Later on, the insurance salesman tells Bill Murray, "You know some of my friends live by the actuarial tables. But my feeling is it's all one big crapshoot anyhoo." These lines aren't something that make you go, "Oh, I get what the movie's about!" But they're thematic, and resonate with reverberations that infuse theme into the scenes and the script without hitting you over the head with it.

In Woody Allen's *Purple Rose of Cairo*, the husband, Danny Aiello, repeats throughout the movie, "Life is not like the movies! Life is not like the movies!" While that does telegraph specifically what is about to happen (the fictional character Jeff Daniels plays is going to emerge from the screen and fall in love with Mia Farrow), in most cases you needn't be so overt and you can simply imply or allude to what the theme is. In most cases, it's better if you allow the audience to discover the connections than if you just come out and tell them what the theme is.

Somewhere in the normal world, somewhere in the first act, you need to imply or hint at the theme.

REVIEWING THE NORMAL WORLD . . .

◀ In what way is your Comic Hero flawed? What is your Hero aware or unaware of?

◀ What is your Hero's initial goal? How is it selfish or short-sighted?

◀ Describe your Hero's relationships, or lack thereof.

◀ Is there a moment in which your Hero reveals a hint of the character they will transform into?

◀ What loss did your Hero suffer either in the beginning of, or before, the Normal World?

* * *

The Normal World exists to set up situations and themes, but most importantly, to introduce us to your very special characters who are going to be living in your world and telling your story.

3.

Dumb and Dumber . . . and Dumberer

CHARACTERS IN COMEDY

"Half the people you know are below average."

—Steven Wright

CHARACTER TYPES AND ARCHETYPES

There are a lot of ways to think about characters. *Million-Dollar Screenwriting* author (and all-around great guy) Chris Soth and I once co-taught a Comic Premise workshop. In talking about creating characters for your narrative, Chris used a number of analogies—your characters could be like *The Wizard of Oz*:

A mismatched group of outcasts befriends an innocent girl, and when given a chance, they display courage, inventiveness, a brain, a heart . . . and also some cowardly comic relief. Putting it another way, your characters represent (emotionally) a child, a teenager, and an adult.

Or your characters are like the characters in the Hundred Acre Wood: Pooh is friendly and kind; Piglet is shy; Eeyore is a pessimist, always expecting the worst, while Tigger is the exact opposite, exuberant and adventurous, bringing boundless energy, joy, and optimism into the scenario. (In *Seinfeld*, for instance, you can see that George is an Eeyore and Kramer's a Tigger.)

The important idea is to create clear delineations between characters so that you don't have four Eeyores in a scene. And while it seems self-evident that varied characters are necessary, a situation I come across in many of the screenplays I consult on is that two or three characters are actually the same person. They're doing the same thing; they have the same function in the story. I see this mistake over and over again.

In my workshops, talking about characters and character development, and in *The Hidden Tools of Comedy*, I reference the **Commedia dell'Arte**, which literally means "comedy of the professional guild or artists." This was a theater form developed in Italy in the 1500s, in which the "central figure was the performer rather than the writer." All the stories were based on a simple premise or scenario and then completely improvised. Every story imaginable was told through the agency of the specific character types, the same stock characters that had been used since the time of the Greeks. Most of the characters wore distinctive masks, and Commedia featured actors who were also acrobats, dancers, musicians, orators, quick wits, and improvisers possessing satirical skills as well as insights into human behavior.

The power of archetypes is that they represent universal behaviors. Carl Jung believed they were recognizable personalities embedded in our unconscious, and therefore possessed greater resonance for audiences than might otherwise be the case. These types, and the comics that played them, tap into, as James Agee put it, "that great pipeline of horsing around and miming which runs back unbroken through the fairs of the Middle Ages at least to Ancient Greece." They included lecherous old men, dim young lovers, crafty, tricky servants, academic gasbags, cowardly warriors and womanizers, simpletons, sneaks, courtesans, and crackpots. Some of the specific archetypes were:

ARLECCHINO (HARLEQUIN) was the best-known of the comic servants of the Commedia. He could be the silly, dumb servant, like Gilligan of *Gilligan's Island* or he could be the clever, tricky servant, like Bill Murray in *Stripes*. He was the head fool in a company of fools, sometimes very stupid but with occasional moments of brilliance. Think Jim Carrey, Robin Williams, or Charlie Chaplin.

Arlecchino was just one of the collection of clowns known as the **Zanni**, originally just a single valet—Zanni (from which comes the term *zany*)—and from which many comic types emerged. Just as Eskimos have many words for snow in their language, Commedia featured many varieties of fools. **SCAPINO** was a more sexual, romantic version of Arlecchino. **BRIGHELLA** (or **PULCINELLA**) was essentially Arlecchino's smarter and much more vindictive, aggressive older brother, like Ralph Kramden in *The Honeymooners*, John Belushi in *Animal House* or Danny McBride in *Eastbound and Down*. Sweet, innocent **PIERROT** was the melancholy clown (Stan Laurel), sometimes played silently, like Harpo Marx. **COLOMBINE** was the Zanni of the female characters. You'll see versions of Colombine in Lucille Ball from *I Love Lucy*, Grace from *Will & Grace*, and Kat Dennings from *Two Broke Girls*.

As a group, the Zanni become a bumbling, fumbling, fraternity of jokers—often in trios. The Three Stooges, the Marx Brothers, those three goofy ghosts in *Casper*, the original *Ghostbusters*. Two strong, complementary Zanni could become a duo: Zanni 1 and Zanni 2 could be Hope and Crosby, Laurel & Hardy, Abbott & Costello, Tina Fey and Amy Poehler, *Bosom Buddies, The Blues Brothers.*

The character who played the lecherous old man, or the crabby old man, or the hypochondriac old man, or the miserly old man was **PANTALONE**. You see Pantalone in Archie Bunker and Basil Fawlty. He often had a marriageable daughter, or a young wife, who often deceived him. He thought he was the head of the household, but that was usually . . .

MARINETTA was the female version of Pantalone, and often his spouse. She could be the battleax wife, like Maude, or the strong single woman like Murphy Brown. Roseanne was another type of Marinetta (with a big dollop of Colombine).

Other characters included **IL DOTTORE**, or Doctor or Professor, an academic gasbag who just blathered nonsense. He proudly claimed to be a member of every academy but in reality was just a pretentious bag of wind. **IL CAPITANO** was the cowardly soldier or the braggart soldier—like Gaston in the *Beauty and the Beast.* He often claimed to be fearless but was actually the opposite. Il Capitano was originally of Spanish origin. (The Italians and the French thought this was a hoot!) Sgt. Bilko was a combination of Il Capitano and Pulcinella. And finally there was **ISABELLA / LEANDRO** (the Innamorati or Young Lovers): Usually the offspring of Pantalone, they were madly in love, but somewhat dim (like Woody in *Cheers,* and Phoebe in *Friends*). Isabella and Leander were the only ones who were unmasked. Except for them, everyone else in Commedia had distinctive masks and costume.

That's important because it meant, wherever you were in Europe, whether you were in Naples or Prague or Stockholm or London, when the guy with the hook nose and diamond patterned tights came out, you knew that was Harlequin, and you could begin to predict what was going to happen. Think of Marie charging into Ray's house, or Kramer bursting through the door into Jerry's apartment. You see Kramer sliding through the door and you're already anticipating the comedy that's about to occur: that's the power of Commedia. No matter where you were in Europe for hundreds of years, you knew who these characters were. They were like watching favorite old sitcoms. Ricky and Lucy Ricardo—you begin to anticipate what's going to happen even if you've never seen that episode before.[1]

CHARACTERS CREATE . . .

So how does this work in reality? Say you have the characters of the two young lovers acting out a scene. Let's put them on a park bench. They're young, they're a little dim. What's their physical movement? Toward each other, right? They're going to hug; they're going to get together.

Now let's say we replace the young man and let's put in Pantalone, the lecherous old man. Now, what's the movement? He's going to lunge for the girl, and as she moves away, he's going to chase her around the bench. Now let's take away the young girl and let's replace her with Marinetta, the battleax wife. Now the chase around the bench is going in the opposite direction. *Now* let's take both the old people away and replace them with the three Zanni. They're all going to run away in different directions but BECAUSE THEY ARE IDIOTS, they're going to knock heads together and they'll knock each other out!

So what does the Commedia teach us? The Commedia teaches us that:

◀ **Character creates plot.**
◀ **Character creates action.**
◀ **Character creates movement.**

The Commedia does this because it goes beyond focusing on funny characters and focuses on relationships. In Keith Johnstone's invaluable book *Impro*, he describes how important the concept of status is in improvisation. In any relationship between characters, someone is smarter than the other; someone is more powerful than the other;

---

[1] In discussing the importance of audiences knowing who the characters were, Mike Schur (of *Parks and Rec*) said, "It takes a while to learn about the characters and enjoy their funny traits. In the *Cheers* pilot, for example, Cliff is basically an extra. It wasn't until a few episodes later that they moved him to the other end of the bar and sat him next to Norm, forming the most famous 275-episode tableau in TV history."

someone is the leader, the other the follower. Masters and servants, husbands and wives, bosses and workers. Status, and the constant negotiations that surround status, are the engine that propels action. The slave wants his freedom from his master, but the master needs his wily slave to fetch the charming young girl who is attracted to the master's money and power, but more attracted to his strapping young son who is a bit dim and dependent upon the clever servant who is trying to evade the vengeful captain whom he cheated at dice. This shifting status war powered Renaissance Commedia and operas like *The Marriage of Figaro* the same way that it powers stories of the nerds and their girlfriends in *The Big Bang Theory*—Sheldon is a brilliant physicist on track, at least in his own mind, to win the Nobel Prize but he often leans on Penny, a not-so-brilliant Cheesecake Factory waitress, to navigate the confusing conventions of social interactions.

CLOSED UNIVERSE

The Commedia also teaches us that comedy is a closed universe. The old man wandering around the streets in Act One in a Commedia always turns out to be the father of the orphans in Act Five—it's a closed, connected universe. If you're doing a college football movie, and the quarterback and the benchwarmer both like the same girl, she's probably also going to the same college, maybe even a cheerleader for the team. Maybe she's even more closely connected to the team, by being related to the coach. In *Mean Girls*, the guy in high school that Cady (Lindsay Lohan) has a crush on is not some unconnected hot senior football star, but the ex-boyfriend of mean girl Queen Bee Regina (Rachel McAdams). Yes, theoretically you could have a speaking role for all seven billion people on the planet, but what Commedia teaches us is that you can tell an entire universe of stories with a finite set of characters.

OUR ARCHETYPES

In *The Writer's Journey*, Chris Vogler writes about the Hero, the Mentor, the Threshold Guardian, the Herald, and so on.

In our Comic Hero's Journey, our characters are slightly different, and certainly less heroic. And it's not just the main characters: in a comedy, no one's perfect.

Among our comic archetypes are the Fool, the Innocent, the Voice of Reason, the Primal, the Magical Object of Desire, and probably the most important, the Trickster.

THE FOOL

The Fool is a character who is naïve, sometimes stupid, and usually wrong about almost everything. In *Tropic Thunder*, Ben Stiller is the Fool. Both Jim Carrey and Jeff Daniels are obviously Fools in *Dumb and Dumber*. The Fool in *Mean Girls* is Karen Smith (Amanda Seyfried) who when told that Lindsay Lohan was homeschooled in Africa asks, "If you're from Africa, why are you white?" The character doesn't need to be a Fool from beginning to end or in all things, but is the character you can call on to be a useful idiot when the occasion demands.

In *A Fish Called Wanda*, Kevin Kline's ex-CIA assassin is a dangerous man, but also obviously an idiot who hates being called stupid.

```
                    WANDA
        Oh, right! To call you stupid would
        be an insult to stupid people! I've
        known sheep that could outwit you.
```

```
I've worn dresses with higher IQs.
But you think you're an intellectual,
don't you, ape?

          OTTO WEST
Apes don't read philosophy.

          WANDA
Yes they do, Otto. They just don't
understand it. Now let me correct
you on a couple of things, okay?
Aristotle was not Belgian. The
central message of Buddhism is not
"Every man for himself." And the
London Underground is not a political
movement. Those are all mistakes,
Otto. I looked them up.
```

Kline's character is an idiot who can be counted on to bring in both danger and comedy in each scene he's in.

THE INNOCENT

In romantic comedy, the **Innocent** might be the sweet, naïve one of the group, like Ellie Kemper in *Bridesmaids* or the Object of Desire, like Rita in *Groundhog Day*. The Innocent is not necessarily the dumbest person in the group, but they're naive in the way that they approach life. They're the ones who need to be schooled about certain situations. In *The 40-Year-Old Virgin*, Steve Carell is literally innocent; he's still

a virgin—at forty. But Paul Rudd is also an Innocent in his lovesick, overly romantic view of relationships. During the poker game that Steve Carell is invited to, after Romany Malco and Seth Rogen swap filthy, graphic sex stories, David (Paul Rudd) shares this:

```
                DAVID
You know, sometimes Amy and I would
make love. It was almost like we
weren't two people but we were
spirits or something. Our souls
were connected in this way, I can't
describe it. Time stood still. It was
like we were sharing the same heart.
```

Even though Paul Rudd owns two overflowing boxes of porn, in many ways he's as much if not more of an Innocent as the 40-year-old virgin.

One of the great uses of the Innocent is that you get to explain things to them. They're rookies. They're new; they haven't been around the block, so things have to be explained to them—and therefore, to us as well. That's one reason why Diane walks into *Cheers* that first episode as opposed to starting with her already having worked there a year and a half. Because how else are you going to get all that exposition in? How are you going to introduce that bar to me? Introduce it through the Innocent character.

VOICE OF REASON

You usually have a **Voice of Reason**, who can be the voice of the audience, a character who says, "But wait a second, what about this? Don't you see it?" They're the one who sees the situation the way it is, but often can't get anybody to listen at first because they're kind of a nerd. Like Jay Baruchel. A lot of times the Voice of Reason just happens to be Jay Baruchel. In *This Is the End*, Baruchel is the one who warns that the Apocalypse has arrived, but no one believes him. In *Tropic Thunder*, he says, "I don't think that they're still making the movie. I think we're lost." Baruchel is the only one who can read the map,

but he's also the nerd who has this long monologue about different game systems and PlayStation versus Xbox. He goes on and on until Robert Downey Jr. says, "Are you talking to me?" Because no one's paying attention to him.

Sometimes the Voice of Reason, the seemingly normal person, is our protagonist, our hero. But it's important to remember that no matter how normal they may seem, they're still closer to the rest of us flawed humans than to an heroic ideal. They see the world all-too clearly, with all its dangers and pitfalls, and if they're part of a group even though they're scared, they'll try like hell to help the Fools and Innocents avoid them.

In the Hero's Journey, the **Mentor** is a wise man or woman to whom characters pay rapt attention. In the Comic Hero's Journey, our wise man/woman is still wise, but because they're a nerd, or a coward, or a know-it-all, they're usually overlooked and ignored until it's almost too late. In *Scream*, Jamie Kennedy's character has encyclopedic knowledge of horror movie tropes and lore, but he's also kind of a cowardly nerd, so the other characters don't look up to him the way they would an Obi-Wan or Gandalf. And even if they don't possess special knowledge, our mentors often are the repository for moral and emotional wisdom, like Queen Latifah in *Girls Trip*.

Or our Wise Man isn't wise at all. In comedies, our Mentors range from the slightly incompetent (Billy Crystal's Miracle Max in *The Princess Bride*) to the positively daffy (Bing Bong in *Inside Out*) to the absolutely insane (Rip Torn's wheelchair-bound dodgeball coach Patches O'Houlihan in *Dodgeball: A True Underdog Story*, whose training regimen included throwing wrenches at the team to teach them to, well . . . dodge). While they offer advice and support as in the most heroic folktales, our comic Mentor's advice and support needs to be taken with extra-large grain of salt. And ibuprofen, if available.

In addition, in the Hero's Journey the Hero usually encounters the Mentor before they go too far down the road. As Vogler writes, ". . . heroes almost always make contact with some source of wisdom before committing to the adventure." In the Comic Hero's Journey, our protagonist is often knee-deep in . . . uh . . . adventure before a comic mentor enters the scene. Miracle Max, Chazz Reinhold (Will Ferrell's hilarious turn in *Wedding Crashers*), and Patches O'Houlihan are all introduced well into Act 2.

THE ANIMAL

Another essential character in comedy is the primal character, the **Animal**. The Animal is the character who is often the most physical and direct and follows their primal urges. If the Voice of Reason thinks only through the head, the Animal thinks more through the belly and the groin. In *Bridesmaids*, Melissa McCarthy is the Animal,

taking dumps wherever she wants to. In *Animal House* John Belushi is the Animal, smashing guitars when syrupy folksingers irritate him.

In some ways, Belushi's spiritual descendant is Danny McBride. McBride is always at extremes. In *Eastbound and Down*, he plays a washed-up ballplayer who returns to his hometown and gets a job teaching gym at the local junior high. Semiliterate with delusions of grandeur, he uses his P.E. class to sell his old baseball memorabilia, gets into bar fights and fistfights, insults his brother's family, and bangs the principal's fiancée. In *This Is the End*, McBride wakes up in James Franco's house the morning after the Rapture and, unaware that food is being stockpiled and rationed, prepares a ridiculously elaborate breakfast (that he mostly eats by himself) wasting most of the food. When James Franco says he can't have more than one glass of water at dinner, he takes the jug of water and upends it over his head. He's not going to be dictated to and he's not going to be denied. He will not be restrained. Danny McBride is going to follow his primal instincts at all costs, the opposite of what the nice, polite Voice of Reason Jay Baruchel would do.

The Animal, when paired with an Innocent, Fool, or Voice of Reason comprise a Zanni 1 and Zanni 2 duo. Examples include Channing Tatum and Jonah Hill in *21* (and *22*) *Jump Street*, Simon Pegg and Nick Frost in *Hot Fuzz*, Mark Wahlberg and Will Ferrell in *The Other Guys*, Brendan Gleeson and Colin Farrell in *In Bruges*, and Melissa McCarthy and Jason Statham in *Spy*.

THE MAGICAL OBJECT OF DESIRE

In romantic comedies, your protagonists may be a Beast, but the objects of their affections are generally Beauties, and fairly magical Beauties, at that. Some have almost supernatural powers, such as Mary in *There's Something About Mary*—everyone who meets her falls in love with her. But even non-magical ones, like Summer Finn in *(500) Days of Summer*, or Andie MacDowell in *Groundhog Day*, or Meryl Streep in *Defending Your Life*, or even Chris O'Dowd in *Bridesmaids* are pretty darn near perfect.

All of our Objects of Desire have near-Magical qualities: like the Philosopher's Stone, that was said to have the power to transform base metals into gold, our **Magical Objects of Desire** have the power to transform jerks or nerds. Some therapists will tell you that people don't change: you marry a jerk, and thirty years later, you have an older, fatter, balder jerk. But in romantic comedies, love is a magical power. Love, and the Magical Objects of Desire that embody that love, transform your jerks and dweebs into better, more actualized versions of themselves. Bill Murray is transformed from a cynical jerk into a sensitive mensch. And if that's not magic, I don't know what is.

THE TRICKSTER

Now you can have a comedy that may not have a clearly defined Innocent, Voice of Reason, or Fool, but you will always have a **Trickster**, the indispensable character in comedy. This is the character who flouts the rules, draws outside the lines, and is either in disguise or helps another character take on a disguise. The Trickster does more than think outside the box—he'll sell the box to some unsuspecting Innocent to bilk a Fool.

The Trickster doesn't need to be the protagonist or main character, but somewhere in your comedy, there's got to be a Trickster.

It's the character who's comfortable cutting corners, living by their own rules and breaking all the others, operating outside the norm. The Trickster practices deception, disguise, and obfuscation. Where the Hero confronts obstacles directly with courage and fortitude, the Trickster upends the situation through fraud and deceit and sleight of hand. He masquerades; he pretends.

In *Groundhog Day*, Bill Murray is the Trickster. Once Bill Murray realizes that living the same day gives him the opportunity to set something up on one day, and then pay it off the next, he starts to go to bed with every girl in town. He asks a girl, "Who was your English teacher in twelfth grade?" "Mrs. Walsh." The next day he comes back and says, "Remember me? I sat behind you in Mrs. Walsh's 12th grade English class!" Naturally, they end the evening in an amorous clinch.

In *Big*, the Trickster is not Tom Hanks, the protagonist, but rather his best friend Billy, who steals money from his parents to stash Hanks away in a flophouse so they can wait the thirty days until the carnival, along with its magic fortune-telling machine, can be located.

The Trickster is Tony Curtis pretending to be the heir to Shell Oil in *Some Like It Hot*, Dustin Hoffman (*Tootsie*) and Robin Williams (*Mrs. Doubtfire*) dressing up as women to get the job or get back their families, Jamie Lee Curtis, scamming and manipulating John Cleese and Kevin Kline in *A Fish Called Wanda*, Paul Newman and Robert

Redford (*The Sting*) deceiving Robert Shaw again, and again, and again. In rewriting the rules and turning everything topsy-turvy, the Trickster is the indispensable, essential character in comedies.

Each of these archetypes should enter the narrative in a way that **clearly demonstrates and reveals their unique persona**. In *The 40-Year-Old Virgin*, the first time we enter Smart Tech, we find Romany Malco stepping in front of another sales rep so he can wait on a busty blonde customer; Seth Rogen describing a raunchy weekend in Tijuana; and lovesick Paul Rudd about to suffer a nervous break-down. At the engagement party in *Bridesmaids*, we are introduced in rapid succession to Rita (Wendy McLendon-Covey), a jaundiced mom with three disgusting teenage boys; Becca (Ellie Kemper), an annoy-ingly sweet newlywed who rubs noses with her new husband; Megan (Melissa McCarthy), a primal force of nature; and finally, Helen (Rose Byrne), Kristen Wiig's too perfect for perfect rival.

In creating our archetypes, we have to remember that Joseph Campbell and Chris Vogler point out that each archetype is a part of a whole; they represent slices of our shared humanity. The repeating characters of the hero's myth may come from our dreams, as Jung believed, but our comic characters—the liar, the sneak, the idiot, the miser, the letch—where do they come from? They come from life.

In comedy, your characters are idiots (at least, some of them are). They're dweebs; they're fools. And by the way, I have to tell you, so are you, so am I. They're human, just like me and you. Characters in comedy come from us.

They're human, even if you're writing an animated feature about an anthropomorphic chicken. The whole art of comedy is telling the truth about humans. And since you're a human, you can start with yourself, and then kind of work your way out to people you know and people you work with and your family. But when I work on a char-acter who's an idiot, I'm not saying, "What an idiot." No, I'm saying I'm an idiot. Let me use some of my idiocy, and let me share it in the story. Let me tell the truth about myself.

REVIEWING CHARACTERS IN COMEDY

◀ Think of a few favorite movies and/or sitcoms. Which of the characters would be the Trickster? Who would be the Innocent, the Fool, the Voice of Reason, etc.? Would any of them be mixtures of two or more Archetypes?

◀ If you were writing a scene in which a character was ordering at a Starbucks, how would the dialogue go if your character was a Voice of Reason? What would happen if the barista was a Fool? Write the same scene over a few times, mixing and matching the Archetypes.

◀ Several of the Commedia Archetypes, like *Il Dottore* and *Il Capitano*, were created in response to local culture and current events. What new Commedia characters would you create in response to your local culture, customs and current events?

* * *

Now that we've met our characters, the next step is to introduce the Big Event, the catalyst that's going to send everyone and everything spinning off out of orbit, when the characters in your narrative go, "What the Fuck?"

4.

WTF? or "We're Not in Kansas Anymore"

THE COMIC CATALYST

> *"What happens if you get scared half to death twice?"*
>
> —STEVEN WRIGHT

Someone wakes up, and it's the same day over and over again. Someone goes to sleep as a twelve-year-old, then wakes up and they're thirty. A guy falls in love with a mermaid. A Hollywood party is rudely interrupted by the Rapture.

In **WTF**, something happens that could never, ever happen (or at least *probably* would never, ever happen). It's the **comic catalyst**, and it gets the party started.

But before that, there's . . . . . .

THE INVITATION

In almost every comic structure, you have an **invitation**—a character is invited or told to go somewhere or do something that leads to a catalytic event. Your protagonist is assigned to go to Punxsutawney to cover the Groundhog Day festival (*Groundhog Day*). Or they're invited to a party at James Franco's house (*This Is the End*). Tim Allen and the rest of the cast of an old sci-fi television show are invited to appear at a comic-strip convention in *Galaxy Quest*. Melissa McCarthy is invited to a strategy session to discuss how to continue the murdered Jude Law's spy mission in *Spy*.

Or, because there's no one else available, Andy (Steve Carell) is invited to go to the poker game with Paul Rudd, Seth Rogen, and Romany Malco (*The 40-Year-Old Virgin*). If Andy isn't invited and doesn't go to that poker game, maybe the secret of his virginity is never revealed, and the actions of the *40-Year-Old Virgin* never take place.

The invitation is the seemingly innocent occasion wherein your character is inadvertently, accidentally, mistakenly, or begrudgingly put into a position to experience the WTF—what will turn out to be a wild, fantastical, or absurd event. This event is at the heart of the Comic Hero's Journey and is what we call **the comic premise**.

THE LIE THAT TELLS THE TRUTH

The **comic premise** is a lie—an incongruity, which John Morreall defined as a "violation of our normal conceptual patterns and our expectations"—that allows the writer to tell a greater truth. Many people think of the premise of a film as a selling tool—a logline, hook, or high concept. It's the one minute "elevator speech" that's going to convince Steven Spielberg to back your movie before he gets off at the lobby.[1] While a great concept can help sell a film, I prefer to think of the comic premise as a tool. It's the tool used to excite your imagination.

BUT FIRST, THE AMAZING SPIDER-MAN

OK, allow me this slight digression.

I'm a comic book nerd. I admit it.

When I was a kid I discovered Marvel Comics, and Marvel Comics was a revolution in comic-book storytelling because up until then, if you were a superhero for some reason, you were just good. You always did good. And you fought evil. You fought evil and you did good. Rinse and repeat.

So when I read the first *Spider-Man*, it blew my mind. Marvel had heroes who weren't, well, heroic. I mean, not really. Sure, they still fought bad guys, but they were just regular people that stuff had happened to, and they were simply trying to do their best to adjust to their new circumstances. Take Spider-Man, for instance. In the comic book, Peter Parker is a nerdy high school student who gets bitten by a radioactive spider and gains superpowers. Now, could that ever happen? (Hint: the answer is no. No matter how many Comic Cons you've attended.) If you were bitten by a radioactive spider, you might get a welt; worst case, it gets infected. But superpowers? No, sorry.

But *what if you did* get superpowers? What would happen *then?* Would you naturally just do the right thing for the right reason? Would you fight evil? Rob banks? Avoid traffic jams? What would you do? Right now, each of you is coming up with your own answer to that question.

---

[1] Personally, my best elevator speech is "Would you press Two, please."

And maybe your answer leads to more questions, which lead to more and more answers. This process of *What if?* builds the bones of story.

The story the folks at Marvel came up with was that they realized that if you had superpowers you would still be a nerdy teenager. You'd still have trouble getting a job; you'd still have trouble getting the girl. You just would be doing it with super spider powers. Simple, yet brilliant, just by working from the initial premise, and asking, *"What if?"*

THE STORY WRITES ITSELF

A few years back, I was teaching a workshop at Disney to a room full of animators. (Ironically, animators tend to be the *least* animated audience ever. They're usually withdrawn artists or computer geniuses and it was hard to get them to respond.) I would attempt to chat them up before class started to get them in the habit of speaking aloud in class. One day I asked, "So what are you working on?"

And they said, "Well, we're finishing up this thing *The Incredibles*."

"What's that about?" I asked.

"Well," they replied, "it's this family of a superheroes, but they have to give it up because it's outlawed, and they have to get real jobs."

Like I said, I'm a comic book nerd, so I absolutely *loved* this premise. "Wow, that's great! You mean, like, there's a scene of them being superheroes and then a scene of one of them being in an office, not being a superhero? And then there's a scene where they're having a family fight, but with superpowers? And a montage of them getting back in shape?" I reel off about a third of the scenes that are actually in the movie, not because I'm psychic, or brilliant, or even a good guesser, but because the idea so appealed to me, so tickled my own imagination that I immediately began imagining characters, scenes, and whole sequences.

The better the premise, the more the story writes itself in your head. It literally explodes in your imagination.

Let me give you an example. In our workshops, we have a writing exercise where everyone breaks up into small groups, and each group has to come up with their own comic premise. The premise has to 1) identify the main character 2) imply what the problem or conflict is and 3) state it in a sentence or two. 4) If the premise actually makes people respond with a laugh or giggle so much the better, but it's not a prerequisite.[2]

In one workshop a few years back, a group came up with the following premise: "A losing college football team discovers that the only way they can win . . . is to get the nerd . . . laid." There was a slight pause, and then room started to chuckle, which is always a positive sign.

Since then in subsequent workshops before the start of the comic-premise exercise, I always share that premise with the attendees of the current workshop: "A losing college football team discovers that the only way they can win . . . is to get the nerd . . . laid." I then pose a simple question: "What are some scenes that might be in this movie?" Almost immediately, people start offering a dozen possible scenes: the winning montage; the losing montage; getting the nerd ready for a date; frat party; setting the nerd up with a hooker with disastrous results; with amazing results; the nerd becomes cool, almost too cool for school and they have to find a new nerd; and so on.

Maybe you wouldn't want to write this movie. Maybe you wouldn't even want to see this movie, even if you were on a plane and it was free. But the point is that no one was suffering from writer's block— from the paralyzing thought, *What do I do next?* We had enough scenes and characters and segments to outline an entire film. In five minutes.

It's not about following a formula. If there were fifty people in that workshop, there could be at least fifty different ways[3] to develop the initial premise. The point is that each person's sense of story and narrative could shape the screenplay in individual ways.

The Comic Premise can be a potent counterbalance to every writer's dread, writer's block, and the blank screen or page that accompanies that block.

---

[2] You'll get a chance to works on this exercise at the end of the chapter.
[3] More than fifty, most likely. My rabbi used to have a saying: "Ten people in a minyan, twelve opinions."

IMPOSSIBLE / IMPLAUSIBLE

In the Comic Premise, we devise a lie, an **impossible or implausible** event. Could a man live the same day over and over again? No. That's impossible. That's never going to happen. But, could a man not have had sex by the time he's forty years old (*40-Year-Old Virgin*)? Yeah, sure. But, would a bunch of his coworkers then unite in their efforts to get him laid? No, probably not. It's not impossible, but it's implausible. In *Enough Said*, a masseuse starts a relationship with the ex-husband of her new best friend and client, and then realizes it and can't tell either one of them. Yes, it's a small premise, but is it plausible? I mean, how many of us have dated, unknowingly, the ex-husbands of our new best friend who always dishes dirt about the ex-husband? Nobody here? So I'm thinking it's implausible. In WTF, you have an impossible or an implausible event occur.

Sometimes the implausible is a kind of superlative, the **most** of something or **least** of something. The loneliest guy in New York, or the least likely person to be a spy. One example of a superlative structure is in Woody Allen's *Broadway Danny Rose*. At the start, a group of comics[4] are sitting around a table at Lindy's talking about the legendary agent Danny Rose, the most loyal agent (an oxymoron right there) to the worst acts in the world. After a few anecdotes are shared, one comic leans in and says, "Let me tell you the best Danny Rose story!" The movie is the dramatization of the "best" story about Danny Rose. Another superlative structure is featured in *When Harry Met Sally*. It starts off by couples being filmed sharing how they got together. And the story of Billy Crystal and Meg Ryan is simply the last and best of those stories. The stupidest pals go on a road trip? *Dumb and Dumber*. The least-likely foreign reporter travels to America to meet Pamela Anderson? *Borat*.

Sometimes the implausible is the Comic Hero's **improbable reaction** to an otherwise unremarkable event. In *Tootsie*, Dustin Hoffman's character is told by his agent that because of his attitude,

---

[4] A giggle of clowns? A neurosis of comics? A heckle of comedians? Send me your best guesses at what we should call a collection of comics to steve@kaplancomedy.com.

no one wants to hire him. That happens with an all-too depressing frequency in real life; in *Tootsie*, however, Hoffman gets the inspired, if demented, idea to dress up and audition as a woman to get a part in a soap.

But once you come up with the Comic Premise—the big whopping lie (or implausibility) at the center of your story—there are a few basic principles that must be addressed and adhered to:

◀ **Once the premise is established, YOU CANNOT TELL ANOTHER LIE.**

You tell one big lie that sets the events of the movie in motion, but after that you have to develop the story honestly, organically, and truthfully.

Big asks us to believe that a little boy turns into a man overnight (which could never happen), but from that point onward, the narrative proceeds truthfully, with no more lies being told. *Spy* asks us to believe that Melissa McCarthy could out-Bond all the other macho spy heroes. The premise of *Being John Malkovich* is that someone discovers a secret passageway to get inside John Malkovich's head. Could that ever happen? No. But if it did happen, everything else that occurs in the story should develop truthfully from that one lie.

In *Chicken Little*, an anthropomorphic chicken incorrectly tells his town that the sky is falling, embarrassing himself and his dad at the time of life when kids would rather die than be humiliated: middle school. The movie culminates in the big baseball game in which our hero Chicken Little hits a home run, wins the game, and finally redeems himself in his father's eyes. End of story. But not really, because that's only HALF the movie. The other half concerns an alien invasion that is only tangentially connected to the story that we've been following for an hour. Two lies, two premises, and one not-so-successful movie (at least in the opinion of Rotten Tomatoes critics, who gave it a 37% rating).

You're not really improving a comedy premise by adding more impossible and improbable, albeit funny, situations to an already impossible or improbable set-up. When I consult on scripts, one of the most common mistakes I find is that a script may have three or four equally valid premises; three or four separate movies in the same script, all fighting with each other for supremacy. The Comic Premise is your one lie; after that you have to develop the story organically, through the characters.

◀ **All action flows honestly and organically from the premise, based on character. Characters determine Events and Structure; Events and Structure should not dictate to character.**

A lot of fantastical things occur in *Elf*, but once you accept the "reality" of its Normal World (i.e., Santa is real, a human baby was adopted by elves, Christmas magic depends on belief, etc.), it's clear that the events following Will Ferrell's discovery that he's not really an elf are character-driven, and all based on his desire to journey to New York to bond with his dad. All the action following from the premise is based on character needs, not on, "Wouldn't it be funny if . . . ?"

In *Big*, the Tom Hanks character goes for help, first to his mom, and then to his best friend. Then he and his best friend try to track down the fortune-telling machine. The city clerk tells them it'll take a month to process their request, so the friend steals some money from his folks, and puts Tom Hanks up in a flophouse, where he has to wait out the thirty days. The WTF successfully sets these characters in motion, so the temptation to "invent" shtick can, and should, be resisted.

Many writers believe in the importance of outlining—plotting out what's happening on every page and every beat, and knowing exactly how it ends before actually writing the entire script. That's how many writers do it, but some writers, such as the Coen brothers, use a different method. The Coens start the movie, and then see what happens with their characters.

I believe the best methodology is a combination of the two. Screenwriter Taylor Sheridan (*Hell or High Water, Wind River*) has said, "You gotta know how it ends. You don't have to know exactly the mechanics of the journey but you have to understand the journey of the hero." But later in the same interview allows that "I think you have to be pretty malleable because the story is going to start telling itself and telling you that there are other things in there that you should look at. And other arcs and other things. You have to kind of ride with it. For me, if I'm really struggling with a scene and writing three scenes to justify this one thing, I know that I'm not listening to the story. There is a story that wants to be told and if you listen, it tells itself very easily." Where he says "story" I hear "character", at least as far as a comedy goes. Have a sense of where your story's going but allow the characters in your imagination to have their own ideas.

During a *Hollywood Reporter* writers' roundtable, Chris Rock commented on his recent approach to writing, saying, "'What would really happen?' And that's what I try to take into any writing. 'What would really happen?'"

Again, the answer to that question comes from focusing on character before plot. As Bill Prady of *The Big Bang Theory* puts it, "We follow the characters, and let them tell us what they're going to do next." Although he's discussing the novel as opposed to screenplays, Elmore Leonard agreed with putting characters first when he wrote, "At the time I begin writing a novel, the last thing I want to do is follow a plot outline. To know too much at the start takes the pleasure out of discovering what the book is about. . . . I think of characters who will carry a story. The plot comes out of the characters, their attitudes. How they talk describes who they are. Dialogue, in fact, is the element that keeps the story moving. Characters are judged as they appear. Anyone who can't hold up his or her end of a conversation is liable to be shelved, or maybe shot."

MIA'S CHOICE

Woody Allen's *The Purple Rose of Cairo* has a great premise: A character (played by Jeff Daniels) in a 1930s movie also called "The Purple Rose of Cairo" is so in love with a girl in the audience in a movie theater in New Jersey (Mia Farrow) that he actually steps out of the screen to be with her. WTF, right?

Whatever you may think about Woody Allen as a person, one brilliant conceit in Allen's movie is the idea that since this has happened in one theater in New Jersey, it's happening all over the country, and all over the country, theaters are stuck with "Purple Rose" stopped in its tracks, with the fictional characters on screen sitting around in their undershirts, playing pinochle, arguing with each other and just waiting until the Jeff Daniels character returns to the movie.

In order to save his studio from this metaphysical disaster, the head of the studio sends the real actor (also played by Jeff Daniels) to New Jersey to convince Mia Farrow to choose him over the fictional character, and have the fictional Jeff Daniels go back into the movie. And so he does, and because the fictional Jeff Daniels *really* loves Mia Farrow, fictional JD sacrifices his happiness for hers and he goes back into the movie. The actor Jeff Daniels tells Mia that he's going to meet her outside the theater that night and take her away with him. The climax of the movie is Mia Farrow waiting outside the theater and, of course, real JD doesn't show up. He's tricked her. There's a shot of Jeff Daniels sitting in the plane going back to Hollywood feeling chagrined and guilty, but he had to do it—it was his career. Then Mia Farrow walks into the theater and sits down, and in an acknowledged homage to Fellini's *Nights of Cabiria*—in which Giulietta Masina is brokenhearted over a love affair and is walking down an Italian dirt road, and then is cheered up by a strolling band of *commedia* players playing flute and drum—Mia Farrow sits down in the theater, and *Purple Rose of Cairo* is no longer on the screen. It's a Rogers and Astaire musical. Fred and Ginger are dancing, and it's transcendent. Mia, like Giulietta before her, is revivified by the power of art, and smiles as the movie fades out.

And my reaction was always, *But what would the character really do?* What would she do if Woody Allen wasn't the auteur, if the character had the will and the desire and the energy to make her own choices?

Maybe from the character's point of view, she's thinking: "The actor Jeff Daniels dumped me, and the person I really love, fictional or not, is somewhere in the movie, inside the screen." If you give Mia Farrow the permission to *win*, what does she do? Maybe she just runs down the aisle, and as she runs into the screen, finds it's just silver oxide and cloth, and the screen tears, and it's a tragedy.

Or . . .

. . . because Woody Allen has *already created the universe in which people can move back and forth from the silver screen*, Mia runs down the aisle, dashes up to the screen, and . . . joins it! She enters the world of the movies, leaving blowhard husband Danny Aiello on his own.

To me, that's a great ending for the character. Not that Woody has asked me about it . . . but if you follow the characters, and see the world through their eyes, the characters will lead you to other choices, other plot turns, other actions because of who they are and what they want.

◀ **Other characters' needs are as strong as the main character's.**

In Chris Rock's *Head of State* (an early effort), the presidential and vice-presidential candidates for a political party are killed in a plane crash[5]. The evil head of the party decides they probably won't win that year versus an incumbent, so he schemes to run the least likely candidate ever for president, so the party is in a better position four years from now. And that hapless, hopeless loser turns out to be an alderman from Washington, D.C., Chris Rock. There's a scene at a fundraiser with Chris Rock glad-handing rich, white donors. Also at the party are his two political handlers. One is a woman, who's in on

---

[5] Always a funny way to start a movie.

the evil scheme, and the other is played by Dylan Baker, who's clueless about the scheme and wondering why he got stuck with such a rotten candidate. There's a point in the fundraiser when Rock, trying to "get the party started," starts playing DJ. He gets all the old white people to start dancing hip-hop (always hilarious) and on the microphone exhorts them to, "Throw your hands in the air, shake them like you just don't care, and if I've got your vote for president, let me hear you say, 'Oh yeah.'" And all the white people shout, "Oh yeah!"

Watching this, aghast, are the two political handlers. Now the woman has a right to be aghast—she wants Rock to lose. But why is Dylan Baker aghast? He just saw a whole room of rich white people gettin' jiggy wit' Chris Rock. Why doesn't that make him smile, or at least consider it a good thing? Because he's not a real person—never was and never will be. He's there to be a predictable character, having a predictable reaction in a predictable way, one of the "uptight handlers" because that's how "uptight handlers" behave. But Baker should be deliriously happy. He should come in the next day dressed in backwards baseball cap and baggy pants, like Bulworth.

There's a scene at the end of *Groundhog Day* when the whole town is at the Groundhog Day Dance. Rita (Andie MacDowell) and Phil (Bill Murray) are dancing, but everyone is coming up to thank him for his help that day, for fixing their tires or giving the mayor the Heimlich maneuver. This young couple, the Kleisers, come over to thank him.

FRED KLEISER
Excuse me, Mr. Connors.

PHIL
Hey Fred, how was the wedding?

FRED
I just wanted to thank you
for making Debbie go through with it
and everything.

PHIL
All I did was fan the flame
of her passion for you.

                    DEBBIE
          You are the best!

                    PHIL
          No, you are the best. Rita, this is
          Debbie and Fred Kleiser.

                    DEBBIE
                (to RITA)
          Hi!

                    PHIL
                (gives DEBBIE two TICKETS)
          Here you go, kids. Congratulations.

                    DEBBIE
          What is this? No way! NO WAY!

                    FRED
          WrestleMania! No way!

We're supposed to laugh at these rubes from Pittsburgh: "Of course, WrestleMania, hilarious!" But the funniest moment, the real comic moment happens right afterwards.

>   DEBBIE
>   How did you know? We're gonna be in
>   Pittsburgh anyway!
>
>   FRED
>   Thank you, Mr. Connors! You're a real
>   pal!
>
>   DEBBIE
>   This is the best!

As Debbie, an attractive, tiny blond, says this, she goes up on her tippy-toes and gives Phil a kiss on his lips. Fred, a big lunk of a guy (played by eighteen-year-old future Academy Award nominee Michael Shannon), sees that, and figures, *Why not?* so he gives Rita a chaste kiss on her cheek. Which Debbie happens to see and which she's none too crazy about. Hinting at years of marital excitement to come, this tiny blonde glowers, grabs Fred by the tie, and pulls him off-screen. A minor character, but delivering a major laugh because her full humanity (and yes, insanity) is allowed to be present in the moment.

Minor characters can be important sources of comedy ("I'll have what she's having") if they're treated as importantly as your main characters. You don't have to give them as much screen time, but while they're on screen, even if they're anthropomorphic chickens in an animated comedy, their point of view has to be valued, understood, and exploited. Because each character, no matter how small or how little screen time he or she may have, has his/her own **distinctive point of view that propels his/her behavior** in the narrative in distinctive, unique, and often very funny ways.

◀ Characters are brought on through NEED and THEME. PREMISE is the engine; THEME is the rudder

If you have a couple dining in a restaurant, then you're going to need a waiter. In *Groundhog Day* you have the protagonist, Bill Murray.

You have Andie MacDowell, who is the angel of love. Why is Chris Elliott, the cameraman, there? Because otherwise the shot would look terrible because the camera would be on the ground since there's no one there to hold the camera. He's brought on through need. There's really only one other character in *Groundhog Day*—the town itself. All the townspeople are brought on through theme.

Sometimes I've read screenplays—first drafts, third drafts, tenth drafts—but when I ask, "What's the movie about?" the writer might tell me, "It's about this guy that meets a ghost and then . . ." The writer is confusing premise and theme. Premise is that weird thing that sets everything in motion, but theme is what it all ultimately means.

A lot of people think themes are like messages or statements, like the theme of *Romeo and Juliet* is "love conquers all." I don't necessarily think that's wrong for *R&J* (although as for Romeo and Juliet themselves, it doesn't look like it worked out too well for them), but in terms of developing a narrative, a statement is a double-edged sword. On the one hand, it provides the answer to the dramatic question of the narrative, but on the other hand, it may just leave you connecting the dots because everything has to fit that statement. Part of the problem of themes like love conquers all—you know, pithy little answers—is that they lock you in. Maybe that answer's too pat, or maybe it misses some important, essential aspects.

To me, a **theme is best expressed as a question**. In *Romeo and Juliet*, perhaps Shakespeare is asking, "What is the nature of love?" He explores that question in myriad ways, through almost all the characters. There's the love of Romeo for Juliet, the love of Mercutio and Benvolio for Romeo, Romeo's unrequited love for Rosaline in the beginning of the play, and on and on. Shakespeare examines the kindling of love, its effects *and* its consequences. A question allows you to freely and creatively explore the characters and events of the narrative.

What's the theme in *Groundhog Day*? To me, the question is, "How can you be a *mensch* in the world?"[6] So, if that's the question the film is asking, the film has to provide Phil with the world he can be a

---

[6] For those who don't know any Yiddish, the answer is in Chapter Eleven.

good person in, i.e., the town of Punxsutawney with its inhabitants. You know who's not in *Groundhog Day*? The President of the United States, because the theme has nothing to do with politics; his mother, because it isn't about family. And Stephanie.

Stephanie? If you've seen the movie, you probably don't remember Stephanie. If you Google "Groundhog Day Script," what comes up is the second revision, authored by Danny Rubin, revised by Harold Ramis, dated January 7, 1992. Here's the URL: dailyscript.com/scripts/groundhogday.pdf. In this version, there's a Stephanie, because the studio demanded that they come up with an explanation for why the magic is happening, so in this draft Danny Rubin and Harold Ramis came up with Stephanie, a girl who works at the television station in Pittsburgh whom Bill Murray slept with once and then dumped. Stephanie, who's into Ouija boards and crystals, is angry at him so she puts a curse on him.

Not a bad response to the studio's notes. But what happens if you put Stephanie in the script? How does that change the theme? If you have Stephanie as the catalyst, a rejected, New Age, Ouija board-playing witch who puts a curse on Bill Murray, it changes the question of the theme from "How can you be a good person" to "How can you be a better boyfriend?" By calling in the wrong character, the theme and the movie itself are sidetracked and diminished. Theme is essential in developing the Comic Premise, because **theme is the rudder**. **Premise is the engine**. Premise is what pushes you, what thrusts you into the narrative. But theme is the rudder. Theme is how you make choices. Theme helps direct the journey.

For instance, in *Big*, Tom Hanks has to wait thirty days for the city clerk to tell him where the carnival is so he can track down the magic fortune-telling machine. While he's waiting, what does he do? Even though he's in the body of a thirty-year-old man, he's still just a twelve-year-old kid, so while he's waiting, he plays. And what could be a better place to play than in FAO Schwarz, right? There he meets a guy who runs a toy company and they dance on the giant piano keys and the guy offers him a job. Because the theme of *Big* is, "What's the nature of childhood? What's the nexus between being a child and being an adult?" So an adult who runs a toy company that makes products for children is the perfect thematic choice. Given the theme, it helps determine exactly who Tom Hanks meets and offers him a job. He could have wandered into a bank, met the bank president and gotten a job as a teller. He could have wandered into a gas station, met the owner and gotten a job selling lotto tickets behind a glass wall, filling gas tanks, and wiping down windows, but how would that explore and develop the theme? It makes more sense to have him hook up with the head of a toy company in FAO Schwarz because thematically, that's what the film's about.

A LITTLE MORE ABOUT THEME

Can you write a movie and not know what the theme is? Sure. You can write three drafts and still not know. You have a great idea, a great character, and you just write it; it just happens. You're focused on plot. You can write a fifth draft or a fifteenth. But at some point, no matter how silly, light, or frivolous your comedy is, it's ultimately got to be about something. At some point, somebody's going to ask you, "What's this movie about?" and they're not asking you for your log line. Whatever the content of your movie, it means something to you and it should mean something to us. At that point, either in your first draft or in your fifteenth, once you figure out what your theme is, you'll want to go back to the beginning of the story and start threading that theme through the narrative. In everything you choose, all your decisions should be guided by theme.

CAVEAT

Is it possible to write a brilliant comedy about a boy and a girl sitting on a park bench talking for two hours? Sure. It's just really hard to pull off. At some point, you face the possibility of hitting that writer's block I've heard so much about.

(OK, confession: I've more than heard about it.)

So while it's not a mandatory requirement, a great comic premise creates an explosion in your imagination—kind of like a creative Big Bang. As the story starts to expand in your mind, you can't wait to start writing it down. When you tell your friends about it, *they* get excited too, because the story possibilities are so abundant. After telling the initial lie, you don't have to sweat or strain to invent comic bits. If the characters are human enough to be "non-heroes"—flawed and fumbling, like we all are, yet keep picking themselves up no matter how many times they get knocked down—the comedy will occur naturally

REAL LOSS

One area where the Comic Hero's Journey intersects with the journey of the dramatic hero is that both sometimes suffer **real losses** in this part of the journey. Mila Kunis loses her marriage in *Bad Moms*; Riley loses her home and all her friends in *Inside Out*. And while some of the losses are presented as absurdities (Steve Coogan being blown to bits in *Tropic Thunder*) or temporary (*Spy* SPOILER: Jude Law only appears to be shot dead), it's important that you allow your Heroes to experience their honest emotions in the moment. For example, after being outed as a virgin at the poker game, we share Steve Carell's agonized and embarrassed bike ride home. Sure, riding the bike wearing his silly-looking bike helmet lands us in safe comic territory, but what makes this sequence vital to his journey, and to the film as a whole, is his honest and raw reaction to his humiliation. We might not be virgins ourselves, but we identify with his pain, and are all the more willing to share the rest of his at times outlandish journey with him.

REVIEWING WTF

◀ Comic Premise Exercise—create your own Comic Premise. Come up with an impossible or improbable event. The premise has to 1) identify the main character 2) imply what the problem or conflict is and 3) state it in a sentence or two. 4) If the premise actually makes people respond with a laugh or giggle so much the better, but it's not a prerequisite.

◀ Now come up with two more premises. Share all three with a few friends. Which one did most of them respond to? (It's not necessarily the funniest one.)

◀ Take that premise, and spend 15 minutes developing it in your imagination. What's the Invitation that might lead to this comic catalyst? What other scenes can you imagine happening in this story? Which other characters might be in this story?

◀ What might the theme of this story be? What's the question your story will explore?

5.

Stop the World, I Want To Get Off!

REACTION–INTO NEW TERRITORY

"For every action, there is an equal and opposite criticism."

—STEVEN WRIGHT

DENIAL

After WTF, there's often a period of **denial**, where your characters simply do not believe what's happening. In *This Is the End*, no one believes the Rapture has occurred, even after blue lights come down Hoovering people up into the heaven, airplanes tumble out of the sky, and evil 7-Eleven clerks are crushed by big air-conditioning units. There's all sorts of spiritual payback happening and hell is literally breaking loose. Jay and Seth run back to James Franco's house to discover . . . no one's been raptured! Nobody is worthy. This is Hollywood, after all. You didn't expect those people to be on the good side of the Lord, did you? But when Jay tries to tell the people in the room what's happened, Seth completely denies it. He says, no, there was no blue light. However, the partygoers start to believe in the end times when an actual Hellmouth opens up on the lawn in front of James Franco's house and semi-famous Hollywood actors are throwing other semi-famous Hollywood actors into the pit to save themselves. (This is Hollywood after all, remember?)

In *Tropic Thunder*, Ben Stiller cannot accept the idea that his director, Steve Coogan, has stepped on a landmine and blown himself apart. Stiller continues to believe that Coogan's decapitated head is just a fantastically realistic prop, and that the movie will continue to be made albeit in a *cinéma vérité* fashion. In *Toy Story*, Woody confidently predicts, "In a couple of days, everything will be just the way it was. They'll see," just before all the Woody paraphernalia is replaced by Buzz Lightyear merchandise.

STEPS TAKEN TO RETURN TO THE NORMAL WORLD

In the classic Hero's Journey, the Heroes cross the threshold and bravely leave the Normal World. They don't say, "Hey, wait a second . . . I know we're on the Millennium Falcon and we're going to go into hyperdrive and go to Alderaan and save the rebellion and all, but I think I left the gas on back in Tatooine." In the Comic Hero's Journey, once your characters finally get past *This isn't happening*, their next thought is *I wanna go home!* Your characters have not bought into wanting to be a thirty-year-old man, or reliving the same day over and over, or winding up in Oz. They don't see the benefits of that. Dorothy doesn't go, "Hey, let's move here, it's nice. Everything's in color!" No! Your hero's first thought is almost always, *How do I return to the way it was? How do I get back?*

Next steps include an often-desperate **attempt to return to the normal world**, to reverse the effects of the WTF and revert back to the way things were. In *Toy Story*, Woody tries to make Buzz fall behind the dresser (the elephant graveyard of all lost toys) in order to reclaim his position atop the toy pecking order. In *Big*, Tom Hanks bikes over to where the carnival was, looking for the fortune telling machine to return him to adolescence, and when that fails, goes home to his mom to see if his mom can make it all better: "I turned into a grown-up, Mom. I made this wish on the machine!" However, she freaks out because she thinks he's an intruder. He then goes to his best friend at school who thinks he's a pederast, until he sings "their" silly song to convince his friend of his identity.

Our characters want to return, even though we in the audience can see that the world they left behind wasn't really working for them in the first place. Andy (Steve Carell) in *40-Year-Old Virgin* is not going to be happy being alone for the rest of his life. Phil (Bill Murray) in *Groundhog Day* is an asshole (at least from our perspective), and we can guess that won't lead to a long and happy life. Rarely does the character see the upside to the "What the Fuck?" event.

But it does happen, every now and then. Tim Allen's washed-up TV star of a long-canceled sci-fi series latches onto the chance for redemption and adventure in *Galaxy Quest*. Or the Comic Hero is so thrown off balance as a result of the WTF that they decide to blow the whole thing up and go full bore in the opposite direction. In *The DUFF*, once Bianca (Mae Whitman) is told that her place in the pecking order is to be the DUFF (Designated Ugly Fat Friend) to her two BFFs, she breaks off her friendships and determines to be a hottie in her own right. In *Bad Moms*, Mila Kunis initially reacts to her husband's infidelity by trying to keep her overstressed life together but following the lead of new best friend Kathryn Hahn ultimately decides to try to be the baddest of the Bad Moms. (Which in the end, actually helps her become one of the Best Moms.)

CHARACTER NEEDS PROPEL NARRATIVE

Once you have your comic premise going, whether it's five actors stuck in the jungles of Vietnam, or it's a guy living the same day over and over again, the question is, "What happens next?" Well, it's a comedy, right? Shouldn't the answer be, "Wouldn't it be funny if . . . ?" Shouldn't we just make some funny shit up?

No.

The correct answer is, and should always be, "What would my character do next?" Even in a totally illogical world, how would my character believably react?

When your comic protagonists can't get back to the Normal World they then attempt to deal with the situation as best they can (which is usually none too good). Character needs—who the characters are and what they want—should trump plot needs to propel the narrative. In *Groundhog Day*, once Bill Murray realizes that he's just living the same day over and over again, he tries to find a cure. He asks Rita for help: "You're a producer; come up with something!" He goes to a doctor, who sends him to a psychiatrist, but neither of them are much help. He winds up drowning his sorrows at a local bowling alley, where he befriends two barflies. He asks them: "What would you do, if you were stuck in one place, and every day was the same, and nothing you did mattered?" Driving the drunks home, he continues to pepper them with questions:

> PHIL
> What would you do if there was no tomorrow?

> GUS
> No tomorrow? That would mean there would be no consequences, there would be no hangovers—if there was no tomorrow, we could do whatever we wanted!

> PHIL
> That's true. We could do whatever we want.

And so he does. With that epiphany, testing out the hypothesis that given his condition, he can do "whatever" he wants, he drives into mailboxes, drives backwards while being pursued by the police, drives on the railroad tracks playing chicken with an oncoming train, and finally crashes into a huge cutout of the groundhog. This sequence is powered by following the character's needs and wants, answering the question, "What would he do if . . . ?" as opposed to plotting the action based on "Wouldn't it be funny if . . . ?" And it's not just your protagonist. Every character, even minor ones, react and create **vectors of action**. A vector is a force that has both power and direction.[1] It's not just the action of your protagonist, or a single character, but it's what one character does in relationship to what the other characters are doing.

While you, the author, have God-like powers and can make anything happen in your story, you want to avoid **top-down writing**, where plot considerations and inventions take precedence over character. Imagine you're hovering over a chessboard, pushing the pieces around—that's top-down writing, where you, the puppet master, create all circumstances and reactions.

But people aren't puppets, they're human beings, even if in the case of an animated film your character is an anthropomorphic chicken (I'm looking at you, Chicken Little). While tight plotting is essential for mysteries, thrillers, and all iterations of *Ocean's 11* sequels, comedy tends to, needs to, shamble a bit more. Yes, outlines are important, but not imperative. For example, John August (*Big Fish*) suggests that writers shouldn't "beat [themselves] up over deadlines." He writes, "My original one-page outline for *Big Fish* is really an anomaly. I rarely go into that level of detail. Most scripts begin . . . with a few key moments and characters that gradually chain themselves together. I'll always have a sense of where the story is going—I can write a third-act scene before I've written the end of the first act —but I won't necessarily know how I'm going to get there." The Coen brothers don't do outlines. They write one scene and then they think, "Okay, what do these characters do next? And then what happens?"

---

[1] Writing about Vector Theory and plot structure in the *Dramatist* magazine, Cynthia Joyce Clay explains it like this: "Vector theories [concern] the power, behavior, and relationship of forces. Each force has a typical behavior, moves in a specific direction, and has specific size or strength. When set in relation to other forces, its behavior will change, its direction will move, and its size or strength will increase or diminish. In other words, a character will change the behavior when she meets another character, object, or place. A character will change her aims and goals when she meets another character, object, or place. A character will become stronger or bigger, weaker or smaller when meeting with another character, object, or place."

But what about being clever and inventive and coming up with great gags? OK, if we have to assign a percentage to it, let's say you have 15% for you to be ingenious and creative and devise all sorts of delicious complications for your characters. But the other 85% is just your characters—who they are and what they want. And that's where the Tools come in.

A COUPLE OF TOOLS

My previous book was all about the hidden tools of comedy. In fact, that was its title.[2] In talking about character-centered structure, three of the Hidden Tools are worth revisiting: Winning, Non-Hero, and Positive Action.

Winning is the idea that **comedy gives your characters the permission to "win."** This is the permission to do what they think they need to do in order to get what they want, limited only by their own flaws and inadequacies. In "winning," your characters aren't trying to be funny, just trying to get what they want. In *Annie Hall*, Woody Allen tries to win an argument with a self-important professor by dragging Marshall McLuhan out from behind a poster in order to make his point. Comedy gives him the permission to do that, and while the result may be funny, being funny isn't the focus for the character.

In my workshops, we play a game I call the **Classic Problem of the Three Lawyers**. In this game, I choose three workshop attendees and tell them that they're lawyers, and that the most important case of their careers just started five minutes ago in a courtroom four blocks away. Then I separate them, and tell each one individually that for some crazy reason, they have to be the *second* person out the door. When I bring them all back and say, "Start," they usually all start racing for the door. Some groups run up to the door and then stop short, jockeying for position. Other groups take their time, looking for the opening that will allow them to leave second. Sometimes the "lawyers" will simply chat about going to the courthouse; I would always side coach them, "I give you the permission to do what you need to do in

---

[2] *The Hidden Tools of Comedy: The Serious Business of Being Funny*. Michael Wiese Productions, 2013.

order to win!" At that point, it might occur to one of the participants that rather than waiting to go second, since they have permission, they can simply make someone go first, frequently by picking up a smaller participant and throwing him or her through the door.

The results are often surprising and very funny. When I did this exercise at DreamWorks, two of the animators in the room grabbed the third one, a tall, lanky guy, and tried to toss him through the door. But Lanky Guy simply planted his feet on either side of the door frame, and despite the best efforts of two (relatively) brawny animators, became quite horizontal and could not be budged. It was a comical sight, and there was a lot of laughter in the room, but here's the important takeaway—they weren't trying to be funny or make people laugh! They were simply trying to "win" an unwinnable game.

The point of the exercise was to show that comedy can be created without directors, without writers, and without professional actors or comedians, simply by characters being given the permission to win. Since they have permission to break the rules, flout decorum, or act in ways that society might label as inappropriate or irrational, they are able to create comic moments without trying to be funny. There were times when one of the "lawyers" would intentionally do or say something that they thought would be funny. It rarely resulted in audience laughter, but after the exercise was over, served as a useful lesson in the paradox that trying hard to be funny rarely is.

The first question the writer (or director or performer) wants to ask is, "What wins for my character?" as opposed to trying to figure out what the next funny sequence or line of dialogue should be. The next sequence might be funny; hell, it should be funny—not because you came up with some hugely funny bit, but because the characters, interacting with the premise and situation, bumble into situations that contain the element of humor. If you allow the characters to try to "win," comedy will occur.[3]

---

[3] It should be noted that "winning" doesn't mean succeeding. Your characters might not succeed; they very well may fail, but their actions are focused on doing what they think they need to do in order to "win."

In *Groundhog Day*, once Bill Murray's character has figured out that because he starts each day off fresh, there are zero consequences to his actions: he can do whatever he wants. In short order, he plants a big wet kiss on his middle-aged landlady, he tricks all the girls in town into going to bed with him, he robs an armored car, and he punches out the annoying insurance salesman. Why? Because he can!

WINNING: DIALOGUE

And while Bill Murray in *Groundhog Day* is doing whatever he wants to (because he can, remember?) he doesn't waste time explaining himself. Because he doesn't have to, he knows what he's doing, and he just goes right ahead doing it.

PHIL

(Sees pretty girl, sits down next to her)

Hey, you see the groundhog this morning?

(She gives him a look. It's obvious she's never seen him before.)

NANCY

A-huh, I never miss it.

PHIL

What's your name?

NANCY

Nancy Taylor. And you are—

PHIL

What high school did you go to?

NANCY

What?

```
                    PHIL
     High school?
(She really doesn't know what to make of Phil
but she decides to play along.)

                    NANCY
     Lincoln, in Pittsburgh. Who are
     you?

                    PHIL
     Who was your twelfth grade English
     teacher?

                    NANCY
     Heh ... are you kidding?

                    PHIL
     No, no, no ... in twelfth grade,
     your English teacher was ...

                    NANCY
     Mrs. Walsh.

                    PHIL
     Walsh. Nancy, Lincoln, Walsh. OK,
     thanks very much.

                    NANCY
     Hey ... hey!
(Phil walks off)
```

Phil doesn't answer any of Nancy's questions, because he doesn't have to; he doesn't need to be polite, he doesn't need to respond because that's what people should do—it *doesn't help him win*. When a character is winning, you don't have to put exposition in their mouths. Generally, the person who most believes that they need the exposition is you, the writer. You think you need it because you think it helps inform the audience, aids clarity, and supports the story. Maybe it does, but the exposition doesn't *necessarily help your character.* You can cut all that exposition, or find the specific time, place, and character who has the need to say those specific words.

For example, in the second draft of *Groundhog Day*, Hawley, the station manager back in Pittsburgh, orders Phil to cover the groundhog again. When Phil complains, Hawley says, "I covered the swallows coming back to Capistrano for ten years in a row. . . . It's a cute story. He comes out, he looks around, he wrinkles up his little nose, he sniffs around a little, he sees his shadow, he doesn't see his shadow—it's nice. People like it."

Interesting. Nice back story, nice color, but really, who cares? Why is this character talking? What does he mean to us? We're never going to see him again. So why burden him, and us, with these tidbits of color and information?

In the final shooting script, they give the same dialogue to Rita (Andie MacDowell) and Larry, the cameraman (Chris Elliott), because they're the ones who have a need. They're going to count.

Larry's driving, and says to Phil: "Why do you not like the groundhog? That's not so bad. I covered the swallows coming back to Capistrano for ten years in a row" And Rita says, "It's a cute story. He comes out, he looks around, he wrinkles up his little nose, he sniffs around a little, he sees his shadow, he doesn't see his shadow—it's nice. People like it." That's exactly what the station manager said in the second revision, but now it's spoken by characters who have a specific and compelling need (to try to cajole an unwilling colleague into having a more positive attitude on the location shoot) and more importantly, it helps define and develop the three major characters and their relationships.

But what about our station manager, Hawley? He's still in the final shooting script, but his dialogue is very different now. Rather than impersonal exposition, his dialogue to Phil now is more direct, personal, and yes, selfish. When Phil asks him, "Can you handle the 10 [the ten o'clock weather report] or not?" he answers, "Yeah, yeah, listen, if for any reason you don't want to rush back, I can do the 5 tomorrow?" What "wins" for Hawley? The chance to do more on-air reporting, and that need drives and dictates his dialogue.

Winning means that characters say what they need to and want to, not what you, the writer, would like them to say.

Non-Hero is the idea that your characters lack some, if not all, the essential skills and tools with which to win. As opposed to Heroes, they're not overtly brave or selfless. They lack many, if not all, of the skills necessary for hero-ing. One of the most important skills they lack is "knowing." **Non-Heroes "don't know."**

That doesn't mean that your characters are stupid, it just means that, like you, there's a vast amount of information they don't know. You don't know what the winning lottery numbers are. You don't know what your kids are doing, or where they are (and if you're a kid, you don't want your parents knowing, either). You don't know exactly what your spouse is going to do or say next. You can hope she'll do what you want, or hope he'll say the right thing. You think you probably can guess. And maybe you can. But you don't absolutely, positively, without-a-doubt, 100% certain know. As humans, we live every five seconds of our lives in hopes and guesses. A Non-Hero is someone who lacks skills. Knowing is a skill. Being aware is a skill[4]. And it's important in comedy that your characters don't know too much. Not knowing creates confusion, mistakes, and misunderstandings, which are excellent ingredients for comedy. Even when your characters *think* they know something, they could be wrong! As Anais Nin has said, "We don't see things as they are, we see things as *we* are."

The flip side, the beauty part, is that the more skills you give your characters, the more aware they are, the more drama you're writing

---

[4] Very few people are paying attention in the world to anybody but themselves. My friend, the comic and writer Debbie Kasper once said, "You wouldn't care so much about what other people thought of you, if you realized how little they did." Other people aren't thinking about you. They're thinking about themselves.

into that moment. By giving a character skills, you increase the dramatic content of a scene. By removing skills, you increase the comedic content, which allows you to orchestrate the comedic and dramatic elements in the narrative.

Positive Action, or selfish-action, is the idea that every action your character takes, no matter how stupid, foolish, or naive it may make him or her appear, your character actually thinks it might work. (Otherwise, why would they bother doing it?) Every action your comic character takes, even if it doesn't "win" for them, is done out of a positive action—out of the selfish thought, *Well, this will be better for me!*

For the audience, Positive Action draws a portrait of the character—highlighting the character's stupidity or selfishness, nastiness or naiveté—and who they really are is revealed through Positive Action. Melissa McCarthy pushing other bridesmaids out of the way to get to sit on a sink is a Positive Action, and reveals the Animal character in its full flower.

A negative action isn't negative in the sense that it reflects badly on the character. Rather, negative action is one that reveals a character's emotional state but doesn't move the character forward in gaining an objective. Depression, despair, anger, and bitterness, uncoupled from actions that attempt to Win for your character—these negative emotions create dramatic moments.

Positive Action doesn't mean that everything the character does is positive, or happy. It only means that everything the character does is done in the hope that it will make their own lives better. For instance, in *The 40-Year-Old Virgin*, Steve Carell volunteers to take his girlfriend's daughter (Kat Dennings) to the birth-control clinic, not because he's trying to be a great guy, but because he has no idea what the heck he's doing regarding sex and he's desperately looking for some information and advice. It's a Positive Action, because it serves his selfish purposes, and moves the story along in an honest, organic, character-based way. The fact that it makes him look silly in a great comic sequence, and ultimately helps him bond with the daughter, is just icing on the cake.

Positive Action is the idea that characters are looking for positive results in their lives, without necessarily achieving them. If two characters are in a heated argument, what's their goal—to be in a heated argument? No. The goal is to get whatever the character wants despite, or at the end of, the heated argument. It's what my friend, the actor Brad Bellamy, used to call "**protecting the possibility of a happy ending**." Yes, you and your spouse are arguing, but you may be pulling your rhetorical punches because you don't want to end up on the couch for a week. So even though you're fighting, you're still trying to get your positive end result, although it doesn't always work out. In my own experience, the worst fights I've ever gotten into with my wife have been because when I think the fight is over, I say that one thoughtless, stupid thing thinking, *Well, the fight's over, now I can poke fun at some of her little flaws and we can laugh about this!* And it's exactly that comment which is the straw that breaks the camel's back, and I'm sleeping on the couch. So even though the result is negative, it's a result that occurred through a Positive Action.

COMPLICATIONS COME FROM WITHIN

In Reaction, complications should spring from character, as opposed to events and incidents introduced solely for comedic effect. In *Tropic Thunder*, Steve Coogan (playing the director of the Vietnam-era film within the film) steps on a landmine and gets blown up. Now what? If I'm the writer, should I introduce some aliens arriving in UFOs? Maybe a bunch of cannibals from the South Seas? While that would certainly liven things up, the better approach is to focus on what the disparate, dysfunctional group of actors lost in a jungle are going to do. How are they going to deal with it, and how will it affect their relationships with one another, and their relationship with themselves?

In fact, **complications**, **reversals**, and **obstacles** best flow organically from the combination of elements established in the Normal World, the upending effect of the premise in WTF, and character. The Islands of Personality in *Inside Out* are not collapsing due to some outside force, or just to throw up an obstacle for Joy and Sadness—it's due to the fact that the loss of Riley's core memories are changing her behavior and undermining the foundations of her personality. In *Spy*, Melissa McCarthy is not sent out into the field disguised, as she puts it, "dressed like Santa Claus's wife," solely as a sight gag, but because it also reveals the low opinion her supervisor Allison Janney has of her.

Whether it's actors lost in the jungle, or actors stuck in a house trying to survive the apocalypse, or a guy living through the same day over and over again, plot and event should not take precedence over character: their needs, desires, fears, and phobias are what you draw upon to power the plot. If you want something stupid to happen, make sure you have a stupid character in the scene. If you want something crazy to happen, have a crazy character—an Animal character who might react to the situation in a manner that creates the effect you're looking for. Events need to come from character as opposed to you, the godlike author, constantly changing the world.

You don't need to make shit up. Once you introduce the comic premise, you need to trust that the characters—their wants, needs, and fears will create more than enough action and plot to keep the narrative rolling along. In *Big*, after Tom Hanks wakes up to find he's a thirty-year old man, he tries to get help from his mom and fails, tries to get help from his best friend and succeeds. He and the friend then go to City Hall to try to find where the carnival is. (Seems they have to get city licenses to operate). The clerk at City Hall is helpful but tells them it'll take a month for their request to work its way through the bureaucracy. So now Hanks has to wait a month, but where? He can't go home or go to school. His friend (a young Trickster) has a plan—he steals money from his folks and puts Hanks up in a seedy flophouse to wait out the month. With lots of time on his hands, Hanks does what a lot of thirteen-year-old boys would do—he hangs out at a toy store, where he meets the owner of a toy company who offers him a job, and now we're well into Act 2, and all the action has evolved organically from the characters—who they are and what they want. In Reaction, character should generate plot, as opposed to plot dictating to character.

EARLY ADJUSTMENTS TO THE NEW REALITY

As characters begin to deal with the new situation, it's usually without showing much personal growth or truth—they're still flawed characters, stuck in their old ways of thinking. Yes, our Heroes are journeying along their arcs towards transformation, but at this point in the story, their masks are still firmly in place, and the progression to *mensch* is still far in the future. In *This Is the End*, as the Hollywood actors ration their food and board up the windows with James Franco's original artwork, they remain the selfish, self-centered bundles of bruised and outsized egos, still stuck in their personas from the Normal World. In *Tropic Thunder*, the actor/soldiers are still gripped by their egos, insecurities, and manias as they try to find their way out of the jungle.

SIMPLE QUESTIONS AND TASKS

In this stage of the journey, your characters are engaged in performing **simple tasks** and answering **simple questions**. In *Tropic Thunder* they're just trying to read a map and find their way back. Joy asks, "How do we get back to headquarters?" in *Inside Out*. Steve Carell tries to work up the nerve to dial Catherine Keener's number in *The 40-Year-Old Virgin*. Simple, right? Well, wouldn't it be funnier if even more stuff happened, more "comic" complications?

Well, not really. These are simple tasks, and they're comic because our Heroes are not, well . . . they're not heroes at all. They're Non-Heroes. You don't need outside complications to help screw things up. These are Non-Heroes we're talking about. They're capable of screwing things up all by themselves.

Steve Carell in *40-Year-Old Virgin* is finally close to getting what he wants—laid. Catherine Keener gives him a big bowl of condoms and repairs to the bathroom to get ready. Do we need a raccoon to crash into the bedroom to spice things up? What's so funny about a guy selecting and putting on a condom? Well, if you're forty years old and never used one . . .

Having little or no previous experience, he uses up all the condoms in the bowl just trying to get one on. We've all been there, maybe not at forty years old, but we've all been bad at something, and embarrassed and fucked up. You don't need to crash into a pyramid of cans in a supermarket to create comedy[5].

Your comedy comes from following your characters in the scenario and answering the question, "If this happened, how would they deal with it?" In *This Is the End*, somewhere post-Rapture and mid-Apocalypse, the characters prepare to spend the night hiding out in James Franco's mansion. At first, Jay Baruchel tries to bed down in the large conversation pit in Franco's living room. Then he's joined by Seth Rogen, and then Craig Robinson, and finally Jonah Hill, all seeking company like scared preteens their first night at a Boy Scouts campout. Jonah Hill even crawls between Jay and Seth and hugs them both as he tries to fall asleep. The comedy comes from following characters and simply asking, and answering this simple question: If this happened, how would they deal with it? How would they go to sleep? It's simple questions and tasks, as opposed to needing to create big, hilarious obstacles or gut-busting complications, like in *The Secret Life of Pets*.

In that film, two squabbling dogs, Max and Duke, find themselves separated from their dog walker, face an alley full of rabid alley cats and get scooped up by Animal Control. It seems that these two domesticated dogs are now headed for adventures in the slammer, like an animated canine *Stir Crazy* (the Richard Pryor/Gene Wilder prison comedy). Except, no, the Animal Control van is hijacked by a vicious rabbit, a member of a literally underground animal resistance league. This leads to a lot of loud, frenetic animated action[6]. Now, I have no problem with frenetic action, animated or otherwise, but if your exterior complications divert us from developing character and

---

[5] Check out the climax of Jerry Lewis's *The Disorderly Orderly*, and then get back to me and let me know how hilarious you found it.

[6] As the *L.A. Times* reviewer noted, "The film quickly devolves into an infernally busy and overextended chase sequence crammed with desperately unfunny comic patter and noisy, pointless action." So it's not just me that found it annoying.

relationships, complications of this sort are better left for later in the story when characters and relationships have been firmly established and explored.

NEW SKILLS APPEAR

In the face of new, disconcerting, and often terrifying reality, our heroes begin to show heretofore undiscovered aptitudes and begin to slowly acquire and exhibit **new skills**. Jay Baruchel didn't have to have any map-reading skills in *Tropic Thunder*—he's an actor. Some AD will tell him where to go. But when all the actors get lost in the jungle, because he's a nerd, because he was the only one to read the

guidebook before flying to the location, because he's paid attention and figured out how to read a map, he's the one who's helping them lead their way through the jungle.

In *Tootsie*, Dustin Hoffman discovers his feminine side, which includes a new talent for empathy and constructive listening. In *Finding Nemo*, phobia-ridden Marlin finds the courage to brave the ocean, and the ability to trust the erratic and unpredictable Dory. In *The 40-Year-Old Virgin*, Steve Carell takes coaching from Seth Rogen on the delicate, confusing art of chatting up women:

```
(Andy walks over in front of Beth.
```

He stares at her waiting for her to
talk, ready to follow Cal's advice to
only ask questions when talking to a
woman.)

              BETH
Can I help you?

              ANDY
(beat) I don't know. Can you?

              BETH
Are you looking for something?

              ANDY
(beat) Is there something I should be
looking for?

              BETH
(intrigued) We have a lot of books,
so maybe it depends on what you like.

              ANDY
What, um, what do you like?

              BETH
We have a great section of do-it-
yourself.

              ANDY
(beat) Do you like to do it yourself?

              BETH
(giggles) Sometimes ... if, um, the
mood strikes!

              ANDY
How is the mood striking you now?

              BETH
(they both laugh) What's your name?

              ANDY
What's your name?

```
                    BETH
    I'm Beth.

                    ANDY
    Andy.

                    BETH
    Andy ... Don't tell on me, okay,
    Andy?

                    ANDY
    I won't ... unless you want to be
    told on, Beth.
              (walks away)
```

Andy shoots; he scores! In Reaction, our old Comic Heroes are learning new tricks.

INADVERTENT RESULTS

Whether bumbling or overconfident, hesitant or headlong, our Heroes' actions often have unforeseen results. Often, our characters' best intentions only **makes things worse.** In *Bridesmaids*, Annie (Kristen Wiig) organizes several events as maid of honor to impress her friend Lillian (Maya Rudolph) and head off the challenge of new BFF Helen (Rose Byrne), only to give everyone food poisoning, get everyone kicked off their flight to Vegas, and lose her position in the wedding party. In *Election*, revered teacher Matthew Broderick talks a high-school jock into running for student body president to thwart the ambitious Tracy Flick (Reese Witherspoon), unleashing a cascading series of disastrous events.

In *Back to the Future*, Marty McFly (Michael J. Fox) inadvertently risks wiping out himself and his entire family from history, and then in trying to avoid that disaster, inadvertently creates a whole new successful, confident, and prosperous family back in the future. As Umberto Eco has written, "The real hero is always a hero by mistake; he dreams of being an honest coward like everybody else."

CHANGE WITHOUT GROWTH

Over the course of the narrative, our Heroes attain more and more skills, and more and more confidence in using them. Eventually, they will transform into more authentic, more actualized human beings. But not yet.

Our characters are struggling with the new situation, but at the same time, they're resisting change and internal growth. In *This Is the End*, once the end times begin, we see bad people being punished and the righteous being raptured. What actions do our protagonists want to take? They just want to go back to the party at James Franco's house, and wait it out. Once there, they fight about who's going to have the Snickers bar. The initial Reaction to WTF is rarely to become reflective—to want to become a different person. There is no thought of, *I am going to transform*. Instead, it is, *What can I do to get back to normal? I liked my life the way it was!*

In *Groundhog Day*, Phil (Bill Murray) is acclimating to his new circumstances. Because of his growing mastery of his temporal anomaly, he's able to rob armored cars and seduce all the women in town. But even while he masters new skills, he's the same rotten person we knew at the beginning of the story. As your characters adapt to new situations at first, they retain many, if not all, their old flaws.

MISSIONS, EVENTS, AND DEADLINES

In Reaction, our characters begin by answering simple questions and completing simple tasks. Everything they do is designed to go back to the Normal World, or at least keep the present world a bit more stable. And then you can start to involve them on missions.

In structuring your story, it's useful to think in terms of **missions** or **events**, finite sequences that have clear beginnings, middles, and ends.

In *This Is the End*, it's the effort to get water, first by venturing outside (no go—there's hellhounds out there) and then by breaking through the cement floor to get to where the water is stored in the basement.

In *40-Year-Old Virgin*, the speed-dating sequence begins innocently enough, with Paul Rudd inviting Steve Carell out to lunch. Soon, they've given him a new shirt and all four friends are involved in a speed-dating episode. Like a well-structured comedy sketch, it has plenty of room for one-off gags, as well as the opportunity to develop characters and relationships. While the speed-dating sequence might be best remembered for the lesbian who tries to pick up Carell . . .

> GINA
> You've got real soft, delicate features. You're very feminine, you know, which is good for me because that would be a simple sort of transition.

. . . it also affords opportunities to develop character and relationships, as when both Paul Rudd and Seth Rogen run into the girl Rudd's been pining after. And as you're building toward the climax, the missions can get more elaborate, or difficult, or dangerous. In Spy, Melissa McCarthy first tracks her quarry on foot, then by motorcycle, finally fighting for her life aboard a runaway jet plane.

Events are also self-contained, but are usually set-up earlier in the narrative, an end point that everyone is focused on, like the performance of Romeo and Juliet in *Shakespeare in Love*, or the wedding ceremonies in *The Hangover* and *The In-Laws*. Events can serve as taut clothesline that you can hang the actions of the plot on. Sometimes events are accompanied by **deadlines**, the **ticking clock** that audiences can follow to track the progress of our Heroes.

The ticking clock (there are literally dozens of ticking clocks in the opening shots of *Back to the Future*) and similar deadlines are your friend. They provide an easily grasped narrative throughline for the audience while also heightening tension and suspense.

In *The 40-Year-Old Virgin*, it's the twenty dates that Steve Carell has agreed to before he has to lose his virginity to Catherin Keener, and in every version of *Cinderella* it's the tolling of midnight, but the best use of deadlines has to be the lightning striking the clock tower in *Back to the Future*. Michael J. Fox is given a flyer to "save the clock tower." The tower was struck by lightning on November 12th, 1955 at 10:04. When Fox is sent back in time, that deadline helps structure the last half of the movie, by focusing the narrative on the one device that will enable Fox to power up the DeLorean and get back to the future.

It's the Big Game, the Big Dance, the Wedding, and the Graduation that help the audience (and therefore you) know where your characters are along the narrative timeline, to know where they're heading, and how far it is and how long they need to get there.

REVIEWING REACTION

◀ What steps does your Comic Hero take to return to the Normal World?

◀ Given the same situation, how would a different character effect the development of the action?

◀ What "wins" for your characters? Is there any exposition that you can trim or delete from your characters' dialogue?

◀ What simple questions and tasks does your protagonist need to perform to deal with the situation?

◀ What new skills does your protagonist develop?

◀ What are some inadvertent consequences caused by your protagonist's actions?

◀ What future event or deadline are your characters working towards?

6.

Hooking Up

CONNECTIONS, ALLIES, AND ENEMIES

"The problem with the gene pool is that there is no lifeguard."
—Steven Wright

This is the heart of your story.

A great stand-up routine is a sharp point of view expressed through a vibrant character, composed of jokes, takes, observations, ruminations, and rants. A great sketch takes that sharp point of view and marries it to a wild premise played out to its wildly illogical and yet inevitable conclusion. A great sitcom takes that sharp point of view, along with the jokes, takes, observations, ruminations, and rants, expressed through an amusingly dysfunctional family (or connected group of characters) locked in a slightly absurd and inescapable dilemma.

A great comic film takes that wild premise and its comic cast of characters and provides them, and us in the audience, the time and space to develop character and relationships and the obstacles and opportunities that will lead to your Hero's transformation and a satisfying, meaningful conclusion.

In **Connections**, the changes wrought by WTF will have our Heroes journey down unexpected paths, leading them to unexplored terrains, both external and, most importantly, internal.

UNEXPECTED ALLIES & ENEMIES

The story is that they're getting the band back together. Or they're forming the band in the first place. Or they look around at themselves and realize, "Hey, we're a band!"

Just like sitcoms are amalgamations of disparate characters that form dysfunctional families, long-form comedies also gather groups together that coalesce in unexpected ways. Like the great Commedia troupes of the past, these gatherings of characters, in pairs, trios, quartets, or more, form teams that unite to support our comic Heroes along their journey.

In *The 40-Year-Old Virgin,* Steve Carell finds friendship and support among the other Smart Tech workers to first help him get laid, and later, help mend his relationship with Catherine Keener. Kristen Wiig in *Bridesmaids* first competes, then bonds with the other bridesmaids. Joy teams up with Sadness to return to HQ and save Riley from running away from home in *Inside Out.* In Connections, our comic heroes who started out in the Normal World with absent or damaged relationships begin to establish friendships, form alliances, and create alternative or actual families.

Former rivals can become allies, like dueling superstars Ben Stiller and Robert Downey Jr. in *Tropic Thunder.* In *Bridesmaids,* while Helen (Rose Byrne) undercuts Annie (Kristen Wiig) at every turn, she eventually has to turn to Annie to help get the wedding back on track. And while there's always a place for villains in our comedies (i.e., Biff in *Back to the Future* or Ben Stiller in *Dodgeball*), here's what you must understand about antagonists in comedies: You don't need them.[1]

Okay, that's an exaggeration. But what I mean is that you need to be mindful in their use. In *Wedding Crashers*, the antagonist, Bradley Cooper, is the boyfriend of Rachel McAdams, and the rival of our hero, Owen Wilson. In the movie, Cooper is a huge jerk and an abuser, to boot. In this otherwise strong comedy, this is a flaw because Rachel McAdams is such an amazing woman, but why does it take her so long to see that he's a jerk? Cooper's obvious bad guy weakens the McAdams character, and by extension, the movie.

Michael Hauge describes the antagonist in a movie as a blocking character, but a blocking character doesn't need to be negative in order to put the Hero or the Object of Desire in a better light. In *Sleepless in Seattle*, Meg Ryan is engaged to Bill Pullman, but may be falling in love with another man whom she's never met, Tom Hanks. Pullman may be seen to be an obstacle, but the character is sweet and kind. In *A Room With a View*, Helena Bonham Carter is engaged to a fabulously prissy, unromantic, awkward Daniel Day Lewis, but has feelings for the dashing, handsome Julian Sands. Lewis may be wrong for Carter, but he loves her in his own, inadequate way. As Paul Feig, creator of *Freaks and Geeks*, has said, "In comedy, you're playing God. There's a temptation to say, "Let's show how dumb these characters are, get some laughs, and have absolute contempt for them. [Along with fellow writer-director Judd Apatow] we share a belief in the George Bernard Shaw saying, 'All men mean well.'"

In addition, characters tend to create their own blocks, just because they're humans. In *Bridesmaids*, occasional sex partner Jon Hamm is a jerk, but he's not the one standing in the way of Kristen Wiig's happiness. *She is!*

---

[1] Pixar's Andrew Stanton would agree. In discussing Pixar's "Secret Story Guidelines," he recalled that Pixar made the following list for themselves: "No songs, no 'I want' moment, no happy village, no love story, and no villain!"

Because of that, you can have a perfectly fine comedy without a specific villain or antagonist. Who's the villain in *Groundhog Day*? Sure, the insurance salesman is annoying, but he's not actively trying to stop Bill Murray from escaping the endless time warp. Or *The Big Sick*? Yes, the coma is a problem, but it actually is the vehicle that brings the lovers back together in a strange way. Because our complications and plot twists and reversals come from within, in many stories the characters themselves can provide all the conflict necessary without inventing an unnecessary villain.

However, if you're going to have a villain, it's important that the conflict between Hero and antagonist go beyond outer goals and motivations; the struggle, no matter how silly its outward form takes, needs to be firmly centered in the inner life of our protagonist. It's important that the conflict creates an emotional, visceral connection for the audience both towards our Hero AND the antagonist. In *The DUFF*, Bianca walks into her high school only to find that the "mean girls" have made an embarrassing video go viral. More than simply allowing us to empathize with our Hero Bianca, we're also led to DESPISE her antagonists, and YEARN for revenge and comeuppance.

In *Bridesmaids*, we suffer along with Annie (Kristen Wiig) each time Helen (Rose Byrne) undercuts her or steals one of her ideas and passes it off as her own. Earlier in the film, Annie suggests that the bridal shower have a "Paris" theme, since she knows that her childhood friend Lillian's (Maya Rudolph) dream is to go to Paris. Of course, Helen pooh-poohs the idea. So later, when Annie shows up at the unbelievably extravagant bridal shower (they're giving out puppies as gifts, for gosh sakes!), it, of course, is Paris-themed. And when Annie gives her handmade gift of all of Lillian's favorite things from their childhood, Helen once again upstages Annie by presenting Lillian with the gift of a trip to Paris. Watching that scene for the first time, I remember that I almost lost my mind with anger and outrage—which was reflected onscreen as Annie goes understandably crazy and destroys the event, and, it seems, her lifelong friendship.

PACE SLOWS

Up to this point, your protagonist hasn't really connected to a lot of people. Why? Because your protagonist at first was caught up in their own world, and then all hell broke loose and they were just trying to deal with that. But now at about this point in the movie, you have unexpected allies and enemies. All of a sudden people start talking to each other, practically for the first time.

After Reaction, as our Comic Heroes struggle with the new situation, the **pace slows** down, which allows our characters to really reveal themselves to each other and to us. Characters begin to relate to each other emotionally, behaving differently than they did in the Normal World or right after the catalyzing event occurs. Characters start sharing truths and shedding facades. This is not the only time it happens in the movie, but this is where it starts. It's where our characters take a second to look at the stars and talk honestly about what's really on their minds.

EMOTIONAL CONNECTIONS

By this stage of the journey, your Heroes begin making **emotional connections**, often with characters they've clashed with in the past.

In *Tropic Thunder*, Robert Downey Jr. and Ben Stiller are both egotistical actors and rivals from the start, at least in Stiller's mind because he's jealous of Downey Jr.'s awards and acclaim. Downey Jr. doesn't intend to be mean to Stiller; he's just a better actor, and so he steals all of their scenes. There's a sequence after they've been stranded in the jungle when Stiller and Downey Jr. are walking together. All of a sudden, Ben Stiller (Speedman) starts to share with Downey Jr. (Lazarus):

```
                SPEEDMAN
    Hey. I didn't mean to show you up
    back there. It's just, I feel like
    we really need to set the example
    for the other guys. It's gonna be
    tough, but I think Damien's gonna get
```

some great shit out of us. Just wish
I had a director like this on *Jack*.

LAZARUS

On Jack. What? Jack? What you talking
about?

SPEEDMAN

Simple Jack.

LAZARUS

Oh, yeah. *Simple Jack*, yeah. You went
all out on that one, huh? You did.
Really swung for the fences, huh?

SPEEDMAN

Thank you. Thanks. Yeah. Yeah, it was
an intense experience, you know. I
just did the work. I watched a lot
of retarded people. Spent time with
them. Observed them. Watched all the
retarded stuff they did.

LAZARUS

Then again, I always found mere
observation in and of itself is a
tad rudimentary. Sometimes, we gotta
dig deeper to mine the true emotional
pay dirt. Thus, we can diagram the
source of the pain and then live it,
you know.

SPEEDMAN

Yeah, yeah, live it. Yeah, exactly.
You know, there were times when I
was doing Jack that I actually felt
retarded, like really retarded.

LAZARUS

Oh, yeah. Damn.

                    SPEEDMAN
I mean, I brushed my teeth retarded,
I rode the bus retarded.

                    LAZARUS
Damn.

                    SPEEDMAN
In a weird way, I had to sort of
just free myself up to believe that
it was okay to be stupid or dumb.

                    LAZARUS
To be a moron.

                    SPEEDMAN
Yeah.

                    LAZARUS
To be moronical.

                    SPEEDMAN
Exactly, to be a moron.

                    LAZARUS
An imbecile.

                    SPEEDMAN
Yeah.

                    LAZARUS
Like the dumbest motherfucker
that ever lived.

                    SPEEDMAN
When I was playing the character.

                    LAZARUS
When you was the character.

                    SPEEDMAN
Yeah, as Jack, definitely.

                    LAZARUS
Jack, stupid ass Jack. Trying to come
back from that.

                    SPEEDMAN
In a weird way it was almost like
I had to sort of fool my mind
into believing that it wasn't
retarded, and by the end of the whole
thing, I was like, "Wait a minute,
you know, I flushed so much out, how
am I gonna jumpstart it up again?"
It's just like . . . pfft.

                    LAZARUS
Yeah.

                    SPEEDMAN
Yeah, right?

                    LAZARUS
Yeah. You was farting in bathtubs
and laughing your ass off.

                    SPEEDMAN
Yeah.

                    LAZARUS
But Simple Jack thought he was
smart, or rather, didn't think he
was retarded, so you can't afford to
play retarded, being a smart actor.
Playing a guy who ain't smart but
thinks he is, that's tricky.

                    SPEEDMAN
Tricky

                    LAZARUS
It's like working with mercury. It's
high science, man. It's an art form.

                    SPEEDMAN
Yeah.

                    LAZARUS
You an artist.

                    SPEEDMAN
It's what we do, right?

                    LAZARUS
Yeah.

                    SPEEDMAN
Yeah.

Yes, Lazarus is having fun at Speedman's expense, and yes, okay, he's mocking him. But up until now, they haven't been able to have a conversation without their enormous egos getting in the way, anything more than, "Ah, you're stepping on my line," or "Why are you crying when I'm supposed to be crying?" And now Lazarus is about to lay down some truth on Speedman.

                    LAZARUS
Hats off for going there,
especially knowing how
the Academy is about that shit.

                    SPEEDMAN
Wait. About what?

                    LAZARUS
You're serious? You don't know?
Everybody knows you never go full
retard.

                    SPEEDMAN
What do you mean?

                    LAZARUS
Check it out. Dustin Hoffman, Rain
Man, looked retarded, act retarded,
not retarded. Count toothpicks,

```
cheat at cards. Autistic, sure. Not
retarded. Then you got Tom Hanks,
Forrest Gump. Slow, yes, retarded,
maybe, braces on his legs. But he
charmed the pants off Nixon,
and he won a Ping-Pong competition.
That ain't retarded. And he was
a goddamn war hero. You know any
retarded war heroes? You went full
retard, man. Never go full retard.
You don't buy that? Ask Sean Penn,
2001, I Am Sam. Remember? Went full
retard? Went home empty-handed.
```

For all his snark, Lazarus is still sharing truths with Speedman, even if some of those truths are unspeakably, horribly, politically incorrect. It's the first time they've really talked to each other.

In *Groundhog Day*, when Phil (Bill Murray) has finally convinced Rita (Andie MacDowell) that he's actually living the same day over and over, they go back to his room in the bed and breakfast. The scene starts off with him flipping cards into a hat:

```
Rita tries to flip a card into a hat. Misses.

                    PHIL
          Concentrate. You gotta want it.
          Rita flips the card again, missing.
          It's more in the wrist than the
          finger.
          It's just gotta—
Rita flips, misses.

          Be the hat! Come on! Go!

                    RITA
          It would take me a year to get good
          at this.

                    PHIL
          Six months. Four to five hours a
          day, and you'd be an expert.
```

                 RITA
Is this what you do with eternity?

                 PHIL
Now you know. That's not the worst
part.

                 RITA
What's the worst part?

                 PHIL
The worst part is that tomorrow you
will have forgotten all about this
and you'll treat me like a jerk
again.

Rita motions as though to object.

                 PHIL
It's all right. I am a jerk.

                 RITA
You're not.

                 PHIL
It doesn't make any difference. I've
killed myself so many times, I don't
even exist anymore.

                 RITA
Sometimes I wish I had a thousand
lifetimes. I don't know, Phil. Maybe
it's not a curse. It just depends on
how you look at it!
BEAT

                 PHIL
Gosh, you're an upbeat lady!

Even though they've had many conversations up until this point in the film, they've been mostly one-sided, with Rita unaware that Phil is simply trying to manipulate her into bed. Here, there's no manipulation; they're just talking honestly to each other, for the first time.

As the pace slows, emotional connections are forged, often for the first time. In *The 40-Year-Old Virgin*, there would be no movie if Paul Rudd didn't chase a humiliated and fleeing Steve Carell around a Los Angeles valley strip mall. Once he finally gets Carell cornered and calmed down, they share a surprisingly sincere and honest conversation:

```
          DAVID (PAUL RUDD)
So, how could this not have happened?

          ANDY (STEVE CARELL)
It just never happened. When I was
young, I tried, and it didn't happen.
And then I got older and I got more
and more nervous because it hadn't
happened yet. And I got kind of
weirded out about it. Then it really
didn't happen and then, I don't know,
I just kind of stopped trying.

          DAVID
Do you want to give it another shot?

          ANDY
Maybe it's too late. Sometimes I feel
that it's just too late for me.
```

> DAVID
> No, that's crazy. You're 40 years
> old. You know, 40's the new 20. You
> wanna spend the next 60 years of
> your life never experiencing sex?
> And not just sex, but love and
> a relationship, and laughing and
> cuddling and all that shit.

> ANDY
> I don't know. I wouldn't know what
> to do.

Rather than pile on the hijinks (Hey, he's virgin! And he's 40! Let's invent ways to further demean him!), Apatow grounds us in the reality of characters connecting honestly, but that doesn't mean that the comedy has to take a back seat or disappear. Apatow doesn't descend into sentimentality or earnest solemnity. His dialogue sustains the comedy by allowing the character, in this case Paul Rudd's David, to inadvertently reveal too much of himself, as Dave does in the following:

> DAVID
> Look, you gotta take a risk. You
> gotta risk it. Look at me. I went
> out with this girl for four months
> and it was the greatest . . .
> greatest thing in my life. Until she
> went down on this guy in an Escalade,
> I think. And, you know, instead of
> saying: "Okay, what am I doing that
> caused this behavior?" I dumped her.
> Stupid decision. I spent the last two
> years of my life regretting it.

> ANDY
> Why don't you get her back right now?

> DAVID
> Because she's dating this pot dealer.
> Stupid horrible decision. But, hey,

that's her journey, you know. I gotta
respect that. I gotta give her the
space. She wants to be some immature
little bitch and blow everybody ...
that's love, man.

> ANDY
> It sounds horrible.

> DAVID
> Of course it's horrible. It's
> suffering and it's pain and it's ...
> You know, you lose weight and then
> you put back on weight and then you
> call them a bunch of times and you
> try and email and then they move or
> they change their email—but that's
> just love.

> ANDY
> Do you realize that this is the first
> time we've spoken for more than,
> like, 15 seconds?

> DAVID
> Uh-huh.

> ANDY
> It's kind of nice.

David is being a real friend to Andy, trying to convince him to
continue venturing out into the world of women. As he does so, however, he hilariously paints himself as self-inflicted casualty in the
battle between the sexes. This is a sweet, comic scene, showing that
sincere doesn't necessarily equal somber.

SHEDDING FACADES

In Connections, characters start to shed their masks and false facades.
Michael Hauge calls this the "getting naked" part of a romantic comedy. This doesn't necessarily mean "getting naked" in a sexual way but

becoming emotionally naked, open to sharing intimacy with another person. Our characters start to reach out and connect to people that they never reached out to before. This is where truth-telling occurs. In *Hitch*, it's the part in which Will Smith reveals to Eva Mendes that he was kind of a nerd and dweeb in college, and his bad dating experiences directly led to him becoming the Love Doctor.

In *The 40-Year-Old Virgin*, Steve Carell takes Catherine Keener's daughter (Kat Dennings) to a family planning clinic, ostensibly to help end the daughter's high-pitched screaming fit ("She sounds like a tea kettle!"), but actually to try to get some much-needed info before he reaches the dreaded "20 Date" deadline.

Driving Dennings home from the clinic, he tries to convince her that he was lying when he admitted to the group that he was a virgin:

                    ANDY
        So, I made that all up to help you
        out.

                    MARLA
        No, you didn't. But thank you for
        doing that.

                    ANDY
        How can you tell?

>   MARLA
> Well, you know, I go to school with,
> like, 400 guys who are all trying to
> have sex. And, yeah, so I can tell
> who's done it.
>
>   ANDY
> Of course.
>
>   MARLA
> And you really haven't?
>
>   ANDY
> No, I really haven't. Please don't
> tell your mom, okay?
>
>   MARLA
> Yeah, I won't.
>
>   ANDY
> Thanks.
>
>   MARLA
> But when are you gonna tell her?
>
>   ANDY
> Believe me, I'm working on it. I am
> working on it.

In *This Is the End,* Jay Baruchel has been trying to talk to Seth Rogen about his new Hollywood friends, but Seth has been avoiding the conversation because he really doesn't want to hear it. But when the Apocalypse finally happens and everything literally blows up in their faces, they begin to talk honestly with each other. It becomes first a verbal fight, and then a physical fight because the real issues between them emerge. Real emotional connections can be both positive and negative.

As opposed to keeping a contrived deception alive, in Connections, characters, as another function of their eventual transformation, can begin to speak honestly to others.

IMPORTANT OBJECTS

Like Events and Deadline, Objects symbolizing important aspects of character or relationships can thread through the narrative, pulling together strands of plot and theme in an unobtrusive, yet effective way.

In *Spy*, Bradley Fine (Jude Law) takes Cooper (Melissa McCarthy) out to a fancy restaurant for what she hopes is a romantic dinner. During the dinner, Fine hands Coop a small box. Is it jewelry? Could it possibly be . . . a ring? No, it's a crazy cake pendant, which Fine thinks is hilarious and just right for Coop, and which is a huge disappointment and breaks Coop's heart. Fine is murdered, and the joke pendant is all she has left of him. Prior to making her decision to volunteer for a dangerous spy mission, she holds it, remembering Fine and dedicating her decision to his memory. At the end, after she has come in to her own and proved herself a worthy spy, she proudly wears it on the outside of her dress—totally owning who she is and has become.

In *The 40-Year-Old Virgin*, Andy (Steve Carell) still has all his old action figures still in their original packaging. Near the end of the movie, Trish (Catherine Keener) tries to make love to Andy, but he's obsessed with not crushing the boxes, which are spread around the bed. "I got this when I was in second grade," Andy tells her. "Do you know how hard it is for a kid to not open that? This is important. These are my things!" Andy is like these action figures, seemingly lifelike but less than life-sized, still hermetically sealed.

DECISION POINTS

Great comedies have real **decision points**. If you stack the deck on one side or the other, it doesn't really give the characters and the audience the experience that they need. If it's a romantic comedy and Owen Wilson is trying to get the girl in *Wedding Crashers*, and his competition is a sadistic asshole (Bradley Cooper) who cheats on his girlfriend, who are you going to choose? Angry and abusive but handsome Bradley Cooper? Even a decade before #TimesUp, who in their right mind is going to choose the violent fiancé over sweet, funny Owen Wilson? No one. It's not a real decision point. In *Midnight in Paris*, Owen Wilson (again) is engaged to a shrewish woman who comes complete with reprehensible in-laws. Does anyone believe that the movie is going to end with Owen and Shrew walking arm in arm down the Champs-Elysees? Again, a no-brainer.

On the other hand, take *Sleepless in Seattle*. In that movie, Meg Ryan is having a meal with her boyfriend, Bill Pullman. We know who the romantic star of the movie is (Hint: it's Tom Hanks), but even so, Bill Pullman's great. He's not a jerk. He's a nice guy, hell, he's a *great* guy. But he's not *the* guy. Meg has a real decision point that has to be made, with risks and rewards on both sides. The decision point in a movie is an emotionally charged choice that engages character and audience alike, as opposed to some artificially created plot-point that is designed to go down in only one way.

Decision points are important in terms of putting your characters in ethical and moral quandaries that pose true questions, and require honest answers. This is where your Heroes have to figure out whose side they're on and which way to go.

In *Spy*, Coop (Melissa McCarthy) is given strict orders by her boss (Allison Janney) to only "track and report" in the attempt to recover the missing nuclear device. However, when Coop realizes that heroic yet dim Rick Ford's (Jason Statham) life is in danger, she has to decide whether to keep following her orders or go forward, breaking out of her self-doubting demeanor and using her smarts and her skills to save the Ford and the world.

In *Tropic Thunder*, Matthew McConaughey (Ben Stiller's agent in the film) is told that if Ben Stiller is killed in the jungle they can make more money off the insurance than they would if they made the movie. To get McConaughey go along with that, the producer Len Grossman (Tom Cruise) tries to bribe him with oodles of money and a G5 airplane. Yes, McConaughey is Stiller's best, and possibly only friend. But he's an agent. A Hollywood agent. So that's not an easy decision for him, and while we in the audience might guess, we don't really know which way McConaughey will go. A real decision point.

DIGRESSIONS

In Michael Hauge's *Writing Screenplays That Sell*, he states that "every scene, event, and character in the screenplay must contribute to the hero's outer motivation." But digressions, scenes, and events only peripherally—if at all—connected to the hero's outer motivation are useful. It's a plus if they're funny, but of even more value if they serve to develop characters.

In *Bridesmaids*, Megan's (Melissa McCarthy) aggressive airborne flirtation with Air Marshall Jon (Ben Falcone, her real-life husband) does nothing to "contribute to the hero's outer motivation," but it does give Megan added dimensions and is quite funny, to boot. In *The 40-Year-Old Virgin*, Andy's (Steve Carell) boss at Smart Tech, Paula (Jane Lynch) sidles over to him in one scene, wondering if he's solved his "problem" yet.

```
                    PAULA
     You know, Andy, I've been
     Thinking about your problem.
     I think I might have a solution
     for you.
               (beat)
     You ever heard of the term
     "fuck buddy"?

                    ANDY
     What?

                    PAULA
     It's a special friend ...
     who you fuck.

                    ANDY
     No, haven't heard that term.

                    PAULA
     When I was a little girl,
     I developed early.
     By the time I was 14 I had
```

this body you're looking at.
Can you imagine that?

                    ANDY
I don't want to, no.

                    PAULA
Well, needless to say,
a lot of male attention.

                    ANDY
Like men, yes.

                    PAULA
Especially from our
Guatemalan gardener, Javier.

                    ANDY
Okay.

                    PAULA
You know, Javier . . .
before he made passionate yet
gentle love to me for the first
time ... he serenaded me with
a beautiful old Guatemalan
love song.

                    ANDY
Really, that's ... That
sounds nice.

                    PAULA
          (singing in Spanish)
Cuando limpiado mi cuarto
No encuentro nada
Adonde va con tanta prisa?
Al partido de fútbol

                    ANDY
          (beat)
Okay.

```
                    PAULA
Whooh! My goodness!
I think we better
get back to work.

                    ANDY
Yeah, yeah, I better
Go back to work.

                    PAULA
Yeah.

                    ANDY
So, okay.

                    PAULA
All right.
          (beat)
So, you mull it over

                    ANDY
Yeah, all right, I will.

                    PAULA
Okay.
          (walks away, pleased with
          herself)
```

For those who didn't take Spanish in high school, the lyrics of the Guatemalan love song are:

When I clean my room
I can't find anything
Where are you going in such a hurry?
To the soccer game.

While the scene may be a digression from Andy's outer motivation (which is to figure out how to have sex with his girlfriend, Trish), it has the virtues of developing the quietly demented character of Paula, as deliciously portrayed by the brilliant Jane Lynch. It's also useful to note that the sequence is almost entirely improvised.

Before shooting the scene Lynch warned Carell that he should "be prepared that I'm going to start singing at some point." The lyrics were phrases she remembered from her high school Spanish class, and she improvised the tune.

So what does that have to do with the narrative? In a comedy, everything.

In *Story*, Robert McKee states that "comedy is the interruption of the narrative" to do something funny. I think that's not quite correct. Comedy is what happens to characters as they try their best to navigate their way through the narrative. So while protagonists like Andy have other motivations that they're focused on and dealing with, other characters, like Paula, have their own sometimes warped needs and wants, and the confluence of the two will often result in comic moments.

So, digress away, as long as the sequence is funny and serves to develop character and theme, if not plot.

REVIEWING CONNECTIONS

◀ Are there characters who can become allies to your Hero?

◀ Which character (or characters) may become antagonist(s) to your Hero? Is there a possibility that the enemy may become an ally later on?

◀ Which character or characters will your Hero connect with emotionally? What will your Hero reveal to them?

◀ Pick a supporting character. In a conversation with your protagonist, have them inadvertently reveal something about themselves.

◀ Is there an object in your narrative that can take on greater symbolic importance in your story?

◀ What are some authentic decision points in your story?

7.

". . . There Was a Hat?"

NEW DIRECTIONS AND THE DISCOVERED GOAL

"Change is inevitable . . .
except from vending machines."
—Steven Wright

At first, Steve Carell doesn't really mind being a forty-year-old virgin since he has so many things occupying his time (Online poker! Tuba lessons! Halo!) but he meets Catherine Keener and decides to pursue intimacy. Melissa McCarthy in *Spy* only wants to have Jude Law pay attention to her, but when she's given the chance to be out in the field on her own, she discovers her true vocation and goes off to save the world. In *Inside Out*, Joy is determined to have Riley experience happiness nonstop, avoiding sadness at all costs. Events force her to reconsider her whole approach and strike off in a new direction.

THE DISCOVERED GOAL

As Kristin Thompson notes in her book, *Storytelling in the New Hollywood*, "Virtually all scenario manuals stressed the importance of the goal-oriented protagonist." In the Hero's Journey, once the Hero Answers the Call, he or she pursues their goal nobly and bravely to the end. Thompson goes on to write, "Yet most advisors envisage the goal as a static desire that does not change across the course of the plot . . . [some consultants note] that there are exceptions, but these involve the protagonists failing to achieve the goal (examples include *One Flew Over the Cuckoo's Nest* and *Out of Africa*) or realizing that the goal was wrong (*Raising Arizona, Wall Street*)." But in many films, comedies especially, the outer goal has changed, because our characters are in the process of transformation, and have changed themselves. They have new wants, new perspectives, and new goals. This results in the **Discovered Goal.**

In the Comic Hero's Journey, our Hero's initial goal is usually selfish and shortsighted. The Discovered Goal is one that our Heroes did not have or even conceive of in the beginning of the narrative, but which becomes an imperative because they have been transformed and therefore their goals have transformed as well. They discover that the goal they had assumed they were chasing (to be a weatherman at a bigger station, to be Jude Law's girlfriend, to party and smoke weed at James Franco's house), there's a new goal worth pursuing. The Discovered Goal is not something your characters consciously seek. They weren't planning on achieving some noble goal. Instead, nobility and a higher purpose is something they stumble into.

In *Spy*, Melissa McCarthy is no longer content with just being part of a spy's support team, she wants to be a badass secret agent out in the field herself. In *(500) Days of Summer*, Joseph Gordon-Levitt realizes that he's been wasting his time writing greeting cards and has to quit his job in order to pursue his life's passion—architecture.

In *Groundhog Day*, Bill Murray's goal at first is simply to work at a bigger television station. When he finds himself stuck in Punxsutawney waking up on the same day every day, he first focuses on worldly pleasures: conning girls into sleeping with him, robbing armored cars, and going to see the only movie in town over 30,000 times. He becomes bored with that (after all, he knows everything that's going to happen) and sets his sights on seducing the one woman in town he hasn't slept with: Andie MacDowell's Rita. Rita, the one woman he can't seduce, becomes the only woman he really wants. That doesn't work out well for him, since he's still a conniving jerk-wad, and she's a girl who's interested in guys a bit less . . . jerkwaddy. Depressed, he kills himself. And kills himself again. And again. And again. And eventually, after being rejected over and over again, he discovers that what he wants to be is a better person, because a better person would be somebody who this woman whom he loves would want to be around—a Discovered Goal.

What becomes important for the characters in *This Is the End* is not necessarily to survive the apocalypse and then go back to their film careers. What they discover is they want to be redeemed. They've been shitty people, and that's why they weren't raptured. They want to be better people.

Another aspect of New Directions is that they actively pursue new **inner goals** as well as new **outer goals**.[1] Our comic Heroes start off their story without much of an inner life, and if they do have one, it's a shop-worn and tattered thing. Their short-term goals are self-centered and petty. As they transform, their outer goals are transformed, but so are their inner goals: to be a good person in the world, to count for something, to be admired by their son, or wife, or daughter, to be a stand-up person, to be reliable: to be a *mensch*. So for Bill Murray in *Groundhog Day*, Kristen Wiig in *Bridesmaids*, Melissa McCarthy in *Spy*, Seth Rogen in *This Is the End*, along with new outer goals comes a desire to be better, stronger, more confident and more authentic people.

---

[1] Another tip of my cap to Michael Hauge, who introduced me to the terms, inner goals and outer goals. Now that you've bought one of my books, you really should buy a book or video from Michael—it's only fair.

INADVERTENT ADOPTION OF POSTIVE ATTRIBUTES

In New Directions come **inadvertent and/or inconsistent adoption of positive character attributes.** Your characters just don't wake up and become great, All-American, gleaming-toothed heroes. They're still the same flawed, fallible human beings that they were before. They're kind of grasping at being better people, and because they're not very skilled or experienced in being better people, they mess it up. They're inconsistent in their progress towards self-improvement.

In *The 40-Year-Old Virgin*, Andy (Steve Carell) stumbles into a fight between his girlfriend Trish (Catherine Keener) and her daughter Marla (Kat Dennings) because Marla wants to have sex with her boyfriend. As Marla locks herself in the bathroom shrieking, Andy ("It sounds like a tea kettle!") offers to take her to a family planning center. Yes, it's a nice thing to do but he's primarily doing it for himself; he wants, he NEEDS to find stuff out about sex. His good deed is wrapped around his own insecurities and self-interested needs. He hasn't become a shining example of a potential stepdad, but he's kind of slouching toward that, taking baby steps.

Even though they're transforming into better versions of themselves, you still want to allow them to stay as human (meaning fallible) as possible. An example of this is in *Groundhog Day* after Bill Murray has finally convinced Rita that he's really living the same day over and over. He wakes up the next day feeling refreshed and inspired. Eating breakfast in a diner, he listens to some classical music over the radio, and decides to learn how to play the piano.

```
EXT. A HOUSE — DAY

We hear a Chopin etude being played. Phil
rings the doorbell. A kindly young woman, MARY,
answers

                    MARY
        Yes?

                    PHIL
        I'd like a piano lesson, please.
```

> MARY
> Oh. Okay, I'm with a student now.
> If you come back tomorrow, I can
> squeeze you in.

> PHIL
> I kinda wanted to get started. I can
> give you a thousand dollars.

> MARY
> (Beat)
> Come on in!

Mary then ushers Phil into the house and closes
the door.

A beat.

Suddenly, the Chopin etude stops.

A moment later the door opens and a LITTLE GIRL
with an armload of music books appears.

Mary pushes the LITTLE GIRL out the door.

The door closes behind her.

The nice music teacher turns out to be not so nice because you
know, hey, a thousand bucks! Even though we can see Murray wanting to be a better person, he's still has a bit of the Trickster in him.

Unheroic behavior can lead to heroic actions. In *Tropic Thunder*,
cocaine-addicted Jack Black has been trying to kick the habit and go
straight, which has never been more vital than in the daring rescue
the actors are staging to save Ben Stiller. In an early draft, Black's
character Portnoy stumbles into the room filled with drugs:

A darkened room.

PORTNOY turns on his flashlight to reveal
he is in fact in ... HEROIN HEAVEN! Wall to
wall packets, ready, for shipment. PORTNOY is
paralyzed. He spots a box with the words, "For
U.S.A., 100% pure, dilute before ingesting."

His mouth LITERALLY waters, and a drop of spittle oozes from his bottom lip. He doesn't know what to do. He gently takes two handfuls of the heroin from the box marked "pure." It's like holding two grenades ...

HALLWAY.

Sandusky rounds up Redyk and Lazarus, points to both of his eyes, signaling that he's got "eyes" on Speedman. They take a step in that direction. Redykulous stops them, and makes a made up, absurd signal for "Where is Portnoy?", somehow trying to mime looking for a fat guy. No one knows what he is doing.

> REDYKULOUS
> (frustrated)
> Where is Portnoy?!

> SANDUSKY
> Shhh!

A muffled, anguished animal noise that could only be PORTNOY emanates from a nearby door. They run towards it. Redykulous kicks it in.

HEROIN HEAVEN.

The gang flies in, to discover Portnoy holding the bags, crying.

> REDYKULOUS
> What are you doing, man!

> SANDUSKY
> Come on, let's go! We found Speedman!

> PORTNOY
> I don't care! It doesn't matter what
> I do! I'll always be a screw-up! No
> one will ever respect me . . .

> REDYKULOUS
> That's not true! Listen, back in the
> day, I used to think I couldn't
> produce a record simply because ...

> SANDUSKY
> ... he's gay.

Beat.

> REDYKULOUS
> Actually I was going to say poor.

> SANDUSKY
> Sorry ...

> LAZARUS
> Listen ... Don't be crazy, Portnoy—
> you're not a fuck-up. You make
> millions of people laugh!

> PORTNOY
> You said my farts made them laugh!
> Leave me ALONE!!

> REDYKULOUS
> That ain't true, Portnoy! Lotta
> people be fartin' and not be gettin'
> 20 large a pop for it!

OUTSIDE THE DOOR.

TWO GUARDS hear the noises inside, head in to
check it out.

HEROIN ROOM.

The guys hear the guards enter the far side of
the room. They can't see the guys through the
shelves packed with heroin packets.

> SANDUSKY
> Damnit! We need to go!

                    PORTNOY
        No, I can't do it.
                (looking in the packet)
        I need it! I need it!! This is all I
        deserve.

                    REDYKULOUS
        Come on, man ...

And the guards emerge around a corner! They jab
their Rifles at the guys and SCREAM AT THEM TO
PUT THEIR HANDS UP!

The guys all slowly raise their hands ...

**Then, in a moment of craziness, PORTNOY CHARGES
THE GUARDS, PIE-ING THEM IN THE FACE WITH THE
HEROIN PACKETS.**

                    PORTNOY
        LAUGH AT THAT!! LAUGH AT THAT
        BASTARD!!

The guards let off a BURST OF MACHINE GUN FIRE
as PORTNOY grinds it into their noses ...

HEROIN ROOM.

Portnoy watches as the white faced guards fall
to their knees, choking and groggy. After a
beat, they collapse.

                    PORTNOY
        Let's move! We got about sixteen
        hours before they wake up!

They run out.

In this draft, Black has a moment of weakness, but then heroically
risks certain death by rushing armed guards with nothing in his hands
but heroin. In the final film, however, the same result is brought about
by allowing the character's heroic actions to come as a result of unheroic
behavior. During the chaos of the rescue, Black is getting his ass kicked
by a young drug lord, Half Squat. He's only saved when they both crash

through the floor to a lower level, with Black landing on top of Half Squat, knocking him out. Black looks up to find out he's crashed into "Heroin Heaven" and finds a table of heroin shaped like the mountain that Richard Dreyfuss was making during *Close Encounters of the Third Kind.* More free drugs than any respectable addict could turn down. A hero would resist that temptation, right? But a comic hero?

A darkened room.

PORTNOY and HALF SQUAT crash through the floor with PORTNOY landing on top of HALF SQUAT. PORTNOY gets up and sees a table ... with a MOUNTAIN OF HEROIN. As he is drawn closer to Sandusky bursts through the door.

> SANDUSKY
> Jeff, don't!

> PORTNOY
> It doesn't matter what I do. I'll always be a screw-up.
> No one'll ever respect me.

> SANDUSKY
> That is not true, you are not a screw-up! You make so many people laugh.

> PORTNOY
> They only laugh at my farts.

> SANDUSKY
> Jeff, we really need to go now!

> PORTNOY
> This is all I deserve.
>   (Grabs at the mountain of heroin
>   with both hands)

TWO GUARDS burst into the room, pointing their Machine guns at the guys and SCREAMING AT THEM IN MANDARIN TO PUT THEIR HANDS UP!

Terrorized, PORTNOY FARTS.

GUARDS crack up and laugh at PORTNOY.

Enraged PORTNOY SCREAMS AND CHARGES THE GUARDS,
PIE-ING THEM IN THE FACE WITH THE HEROIN.

                      PORTNOY
      Laugh at that, you bastards! Oh,
      hilarious! Hilarious!
             (to SANDUSKY)
      Let's move! We only have sixteen
      hours before they wake up!

They run out.

Jack Black's heroism doesn't come about because he's been transformed into a classic Hero; his actions are a result of his unique flaws and regret, not in spite of it. Even as they transform, make sure your characters' adoption of positive character attributes are either inadvertent or inconsistent, or preferably, both.

As your characters find new goals and go in new directions, the trap you want to avoid is to suddenly make them perfect. Don't make them saints; none of us are saints. None of us are perfect. Creating a character who abruptly becomes perfect is telling a lie and remember: comedy tells the truth.

REVIEWING NEW DIRECTIONS

◀ What is the Discovered Goal for your Hero? How does this differ from the Initial Goal, and what does it tell you about your Hero's growth?

◀ What are some positive attributes your Hero has developed? How is your Hero still flawed and fallible, given these positive attributes?

◀ Imagine a character performing a heroic act in an unheroic fashion.

8.

Lost at Sea

DISCONNECTIONS

"Black holes are where God divided by zero."
—STEVEN WRIGHT

ALL IS LOST

Disconnection is the lowest point in the narrative. It's where success for the Hero is at its least likely stage, and the outcome is truly in doubt. Even if you absolutely know there's going to be an all-around happy ending (after all, this is a comedy, and probably a big-budget, Hollywood studio comedy, to boot), you have absolutely no idea how they're going wriggle out of this one. How is this ever going to turn out right? Alliances crumble, friendships end, enterprises go bust, all hope is lost. The Hero appears defeated, or seems to give up, or retreats back into a shell. This is **the long dark night of the soul**.

RELATIONSHIPS COME APART

In romantic comedies, we expect the couple to break up at a certain point in the narrative: Sally leaves Harry, Summer (Zoey Deschanel) leaves Joseph Gordon-Levitt, Alvy Singer (Woody Allen) and Annie Hall (Diane Keaton) break up. In *Tootsie*, Dustin Hoffman loses his best friend (Terri Garr), his role on a soap opera, the girl of his dreams, and the girl of his dreams' father, all at the same time.

But there are disconnections and ruptures beyond romantic ones. In *Inside Out*, Joy abandons Sadness, only to plunge into the inescapable Memory Dump, with no apparent way out. In *Tropic Thunder*, the platoon literally disconnects when the idiotic Ben Stiller, convinced that his director (the blown-to-smithereens Steve Coogan) is alive and well and surreptitiously filming the movie with secret cameras planted everywhere, resolves to go it alone as the rest of the actor-soldiers move in the opposite direction to try to make it back to the base camp. He's walking through swamps, through jungle, imagining he's still shooting this movie. He is literally disconnected from everybody else. In *Bad Moms*, Mila Kunis loses her job, and the love and affection of her two kids and her dog. After Kristen Wiig's complete meltdown at Maya Rudolph's bridal shower in *Bridesmaids*, these BFFs are officially OFF. In addition, she loses her apartment, her car gets totaled, and she breaks up with her policeman boyfriend (Chris O'Dowd).

This occurs about three-quarters of the way through *Bridesmaids*, as do many Disconnections, but actually, this stage of the journey can happen at many different points in the narrative. In the fractal storytelling of *(500) Days of Summer*, the depression is first encountered about five minutes into the movie. Bill Murray's long, dark night of the soul occurs about halfway through *Groundhog Day*. And the breakup of the platoon in *Tropic Thunder* occurs less than halfway through the movie.

THE MASK IS PUT BACK ON

As friendships and couples break up, our menschen, for the moment, put their masks back on. In *Dodgeball: A True Underdog Story*, there's a moment where it looks like the protagonist Peter La Fleur (Vince Vaughn) has taken a payoff to throw the game and let Ben Stiller's team win the tournament. When his anxious team asks what the plan is he replies:

```
                PETER
    What do you guys want from me?
    I don't have a plan for you.
    We're gonna play Globo Gym tomorrow
    and we're probably gonna lose.
    It's the truth. The sooner you guys
    get that through your head, the
    easier this will all be.
```

In crushing his team's hopes (he physically grabs Steve the Pirate [Alan Tudyk], telling him he's not a pirate and sending Steve into a non-pirate existential funk) he's put back on his mask of being the lazy, selfish, uncaring Vince Vaughn that we saw in the beginning of the movie.

In *Groundhog Day*, as Bill Murray struggles with the depressing realization that he'll never escape reliving the same day over and over, he reverts to the cynical jerk he had been evolving from.

```
EXT. GOBBLER'S KNOB — DAWN

The crowd is waiting expectantly for the
groundhog to appear

Phil is a wreck.

                PHIL
    This is pitiful. 1,000 people
    freezing their butts off waiting to
    worship a rat. Groundhog Day used
    to mean something in this town. They
    used to pull the hog out and eat it.
```

```
              (TO THE CROWD)
        You're hypocrites, all of you!
(RITA and LARRY looked shocked)
        You got a problem with what I'm
        saying, Larry? Untie your tongue.
        Come here and talk.
              (to RITA)
        Am I upsetting you, Princess?
(RITA doesn't know how to respond)
```

Suffering real pain, Murray slips his nasty mask back on.

In *The 40-Year-Old Virgin*, the Disconnection starts with a fight between Andy (Steve Carell) and Trish (Catherine Keener). Calculating that they've finally reached the twenty-date mark, Trish says, "I just think we should just go crazy on each other!" and throws herself at him. In doing so, they roll over on several of his action figures. He gets upset, ostensibly because they're damaging the packaging, thus endangering the value, but in fact he's upset because his world (the Normal World) is rapidly coming to an end. He's about to enter into a new world, and it scares him.

```
               ANDY
     I gotta pick those up.
```

                    TRISH
Don't pick them up now.

                    ANDY
No, I have to pick those up
right now.

                    TRISH
Wait, we'll get them later.

                    ANDY
Listen, no, I can't, no.
Listen, it's really important because
once the integrity of the box gets
compromised ... This is original
packaging and that's why these things
are so valuable. So you don't screw
with that. You really don't screw
with that.

                    TRISH
All right. We can wrap them again
later, you know.

                    ANDY
Yeah, I know. But you know what,
this is very important that we don't
lose the value and compromise
the integrity of it.

                    TRISH
Andy, I'm throwing myself at you and
all you can think about is a fucking
toy.

                    ANDY
They're not fucking toys! This is
Iron Man, okay? I got this when I
was in second grade. Do you know how
hard it is for a kid to not open
that? This is important. These are my
things and you are trying to make me
sell them and I don't want to.

Andy starts the movie as the poster child for arrested development. Just like his Iron Man doll, he's been in his original packaging for years. With the help of Trish and the well-intentioned, somewhat blundering efforts of his three coworkers, Andy has been transforming his life and his relationships, evolving into an adult. But now, the mask is put back on again, as Andy **regresses** and retreats back into his safe packaging.

                    ANDY
          And you're making me.

                    TRISH
          I'm not making ...

                    ANDY
          You are encouraging me to quit my
          job.

                    TRISH
          I'm not! I'm not trying to ...

                    ANDY
          You want me to open a store.
          You want me to sell everything.
          You know what, I'm gonna tell you
          something. I don't just change like
          that. I can't just change for you.

                    TRISH
          I don't ... I'm not trying
          to change you. I like you.
          I'm just ... I'm trying
          to help you grow up, Andy.

                    ANDY
          Well, thanks ... a lot!

                    TRISH
          I mean, my God, you ride a bicycle
          to work in a stockroom.

THE COMIC HERO'S JOURNEY   ⏺   KAPLAN

                    ANDY
You know what, I'm not
in the stockroom anymore.
I'm a floor manager!

                    TRISH
Okay.

                    ANDY
And I ride a bike because I like to.
Einstein rode a bike.

                    TRISH
He had a wife who he fucked,
by the way. (BEAT) What do I have to
do for you to have sex with me?
Do you want me to dress up like
Thor? I'll dress up like Thor.
I'll dress up like Iron Man.
What do they do? I'll do it.

                    ANDY
What? Everything's always
about sex.

                    TRISH
Why don't you want to have sex with
me? Why not? Tell me. You tell me
the truth. Is it because I have a
kid who has a kid? Is that why?

                    ANDY
No, it's cool that you're a
grandmother. I love the fact that
you're a grandmother.

                    TRISH
Oh, God!

                    ANDY
You are. You're a hot grandma.

                    TRISH
Oh, my God! You are so mean!

The things that Trish and Andy say to solve the problem ("Do you want me to dress up like Thor? I'll dress up like Thor." "It's cool that you're a grandmother. I love the fact that you're a grandmother.") actually make matters worse. This is an example of **Positive Action**—your characters doing and saying things that they think will help (even if they don't). Andy's declaration that he loves that Trish is a "hot grandma" is said with the best of intentions, even if it has the completely opposite result.

```
                    TRISH
        Get out!

                    ANDY
        Okay, fine. Good!

                    TRISH
        Good, fine. You're gonna go.

                    ANDY
        I didn't ask for any of this.

                    TRISH
        You asked for all of it, Andy.
```

Andy backs away from his transformation, and replaces the mask, as though to revert back to his adolescent-like life in the Normal World. He can't completely turn the clock back, though, because of the transformations that have already occurred.

ABANDON ALL HOPE

There seems to be no way that our Heroes will come out of this one. In *Tootsie*, Dustin Hoffman is trapped. He's declared his love for his soap-opera costar, Jessica Lange while dressed as his alter ego, Dorothy. Attracted but confused, Lange rejects him, especially since her dad (Charles Durning) had already proposed to Dorothy. On top of that, the producers want to extend Dorothy's contract for another year. How to extricate himself, get the girl, keep his career, and not get arrested for fraud?

In *Silver Linings Playbook*, Bradley Cooper, Jennifer Lawrence, Robert De Niro, and the Philadelphia Eagles have to win an impossible parlay to win back De Niro's money, but moments before the big dance competition, Lawrence decides that it's pointless, and gives up and goes to the bar to drink. In *Finding Nemo*, Marlin (Albert Brooks) has swum across an entire ocean to rescue Nemo (Alexander Gould), only to leave Sydney empty-handed, convinced that his son is dead.

This time, it looks like the heroes won't win. This time, there won't be a happy ending. Yes, for the most part, it's a con, but your goal is to make the audience think, *How is this ever going to turn out well?* Often the worse you make the heroes chances, the better the Act 3 will be.

REAL LOSS

The setbacks in Disconnections go beyond marital breakups. Real losses are involved, refuting the myth that no one in a comedy gets hurt. In *Bridesmaids*, Annie (Kristen Wiig) loses her boyfriend, her job, her apartment, and her best friend. In *Four Weddings and a Funeral*, Hugh Grant's best friend Gareth (Simon Callow) suffers a heart attack and dies. In *Groundhog Day*, Bill Murray kills himself. Over and over and over.

But just like the folks in 12-step groups have told us, after hitting bottom, there's nowhere else to go but up. The pain of loss and reversals leads to our characters finally coming to grips with who they are, where they are, and where they have to go. In *(500) Days of Summer*, losing Summer leads Tom to quit the dead-end job at the greeting card company and reinvest in his dream of being an architect. The futility of repeatedly killing himself, only to wake to the same pointless and shallow life, leads Bill Murray in *Groundhog Day* to stop living a selfish existence and start caring about others. And the constant body blows suffered by Kristen Wiig in *Bridesmaids* leads her, at her most vulnerable, to find the self-respect to finally reject the caddish Jon Hamm.

TRAGEDY OR COMEDY?

It's a comedy. How serious should we be in Disconnections?

As W.C. Fields once said, "Pathos is the true base of all laughter." For us to laugh, we have to care, even in the silliest spoof like *Airplane!* Life is a combination of the dramatic and the comedic, the tragic and the absurd, and every great comedy has some combination of these elements. I can think of many dramas that have no comedy in them, but I'm hard-pressed to think of a great comedy that lacks a dramatic thread.

In designing sequences for this section, remember that the tragic and the absurd are often two sides of the same coin. In *Groundhog Day,* in the scenes leading up to Phil's numerous suicide attempts, the writers Harold Ramis and Danny Rubin intersperse scenes of stark depression with absurdist, silly humor. The scene in which Phil stares into the camera and says mournfully, "It's cold out there, campers; it's cold out there, every day," is followed by the scene in which Phil is watching *Jeopardy!* in his pajamas and answering all the questions before they're even asked while drinking scotch straight out of the bottle, freaking out his poor landlady, which is followed by another scene of bleak despair:

```
                    PHIL
     You know, you want a prediction
     about the weather you're asking the
     wrong Phil. I'll give you a winter
     prediction.
     It's going to be cold...
     It's going to be gray ...
     And it's going to last you for the
     rest of your life.
```

How serious should you be? As serious, and as dramatic, as your story and the characters require. Life is painful at time, and that's the truth. Telling the truth about characters, especially when it's a painful truth, allows us to connect emotionally to our characters and eventually experience true redemption and catharsis.

REVIEWING DISCONNECTIONS

◀ What has your Comic Hero lost by this point in your story? How has your Hero suffered?

◀ In what way has your Hero regressed? How is it similar to who your Hero was in the Normal World?

◀ What irresolvable or impossible problems does your Hero face at this point in the story?

9.

"Who Ya Gonna Call?"

RACING TO THE FINISH

"The early bird gets the worm, but the second mouse gets the cheese."
—STEVEN WRIGHT

Whether it's Billy Crystal running through Manhattan to get to the New Year's Eve party in time in *When Harry Met Sally*, or Steve Carell pedaling after Catherine Keener on his bike in *The 40-Year-Old Virgin*, or Bradley Cooper, Ed Helms, Zach Galifianakis, and Justin Bartha racing back from Vegas to Bartha's wedding in *The Hangover*, your characters are desperately scrambling, trying to avoid disaster and, for once in their lives, not snatch defeat from the jaws of victory as they **Race to the Finish**.

RE-INVITATION

Just like an invitation is often essential in setting your protagonists off on their comic journey, a **re-invitation** is required to provide them with the necessary spark following the depths of Disconnections. Bing Bong shows Joy the way out of the Memory Dump in *Inside Out*, even sacrificing himself to help her escape, and all three of Andy's (Steve Carell) friends from the electronics store converge on Beth's (Elizabeth Banks) bathroom to help Andy go back to Trish and avoid making the biggest mistake of his life. In *Bridesmaids*, Megan (Melissa McCarthy) literally pushes Annie (Kristin Wiig) off the couch to help get her out of her depression:

> MEGAN
> But you wouldn't know
> anything about that,
> because you haven't
> been returning my calls.
>
> ANNIE
> And say what, Megan?
> Say, "Hi, I can't
> get off the couch.
> I got fired from my job.
> I got kicked out
> of my apartment.
> I can't pay any of my bills.
> My car is a piece of shit.
> I don't have any friends.
> The last time I ..."
>
> MEGAN
> You know what I
> find interesting
> about that, Annie?
> It's interesting to me
> that you have
> absolutely no friends.
> You know why
> it's interesting?

Here's a friend
standing directly
in front of you,
trying to talk to you.
And you choose to
talk about the fact
that you don't
have any friends.

                    ANNIE
You know what I mean.

                    MEGAN
No, I don't think
you want any help.
I think you want to
have a little pity party.
          (pokes ANNIE)

                    ANNIE
That's not true.

                    MEGAN
          (poking her)
I think Annie wants
a little pity party.
You're an asshole, Annie!
          (pushes ANNIE)

                    ANNIE
Oh, my God.
What are you doing?

                    MEGAN
        You're an asshole. I'm life.
                (pushes her)
        Is life bothering you?

                    ANNIE
        Yes! What are you doing?

                    MEGAN
        I'm life, Annie.
        I'm life, Annie.
        You have got to
        fight back on life.

                    ANNIE
        Megan!

                    MEGAN
        You better learn to fight.

                    ANNIE
        Megan!

                    MEGAN
                (wrestling her)
        I'm life and I'm going
        to bite you in the ass!
                (BITES her)

                    ANNIE
                (SCREAMING)
        Ow! Megan ...

                    MEGAN
        It's not me.
        I'm your life. Turn over!

                    ANNIE
        My God!

                    MEGAN
        I'm trying to get you to fight
        for your shitty life,
        and you won't do it!

```
                    (slaps her)
You just won't do it.

                    ANNIE
Stop it.

                    MEGAN
          (slapping ANNIE with her own
          hand)
You stop slapping yourself.
Stop slapping yourself.
I'm your life, Annie.
I'm your shitty ...
               (ANNIE slaps MEGAN off of her)

                    ANNIE
I'm sorry.

                    MEGAN
Nice hit.
All right.
I'm glad to see
you've got a little
bit of spark in you.
I knew that Annie
was in there somewhere.
```

Coming out of Disconnections, our comic Heroes often need a helpful shove (or a really hard slap) to get them back on track at the end.

SUCCESS / FAILURE = HAIR'S BREADTH

As in action or thriller films, the most effective successes are those in which failure is averted by the narrowest of margins. You have a ticking clock and you only have seconds left. Even though the fate of the universe might not be hanging in the balance, the events in a comic narrative should also be a matter of life or death for our characters. All evidence should point to the fact that there's no way our Hero could possible prevail. Billy Crystal barely makes it to the New Year's party in time to declare his love for Meg Ryan; Buddy the Elf (Will Ferrell) has to convince his whole (step-) family and a crowd of jaded, cynical New Yorkers to believe in Christmas once again in a last-ditch effort to save the holiday. In *The Graduate*, Benjamin (Dustin Hoffman) impossibly races from Berkeley to Pasadena, then back to Berkeley, and then to Santa Monica to try to stop Elaine (Katherine Ross) from getting married. Stopping at a gas station, he calls the groom's father's answering service:

>   BENJAMIN
> Hello, who is this?
>
>   ANSWERING SERVICE
> This is Dr. Smith's answering.
>
>   BENJAMIN
> Is the doctor anywhere?
>
>   ANSWERING SERVICE
> Well, I'm afraid the doctor
> can't be reached right now. If
> you'd like to leave ...
>
>   BENJAMIN
> I have to know where he is.
>
>   ANSWERING SERVICE
> Well, you see, the doctor's at his
> son's wedding, but I'm sure it's over
> by now.

It's almost physically impossible to have driven that far, that fast, and Benjamin is still going to be too late. There's almost no physical way that he can make it in time. But he does make it at the very end. Just like Indiana Jones sliding underneath a huge boulder threatening to crush him or block his way when there literally is no room to slide, our Hero magically, impossibly, averts disaster at, if not past, the very last minute. If you make audiences desperately want your Heroes to win while thinking there's no way in the world that can happen, when it does happen, there's going to be a huge release of endorphins.

Some comedies tell stories about times in which victory is not snatched from defeat's jaws, such as *The Break-Up* and *My Best*

Friend's Wedding. In those cases, however, our disappointment is leavened by the pleasant surprise of the reversal along with the strong thematic and emotional experience delivered. The failure to achieve their goals were paradoxically also successes in a way, and in the end seemed appropriate and ultimately satisfying.

ACTIVE PROTAGONIST

Race to the Finish is often an actual race, either on foot, on bike, or in a car. However, I've read too many scripts where the action has been doled out to other characters and the protagonist is passive at the end of the narrative. I remember reading a script, a really good romantic comedy where at the end, the protagonist did nothing. It all kind of resolved without him. That's not the best choice because, even if it's small, your character **has to take an action to make something happen**. At this point in the movie you cannot afford a passive protagonist.

What's important here is that your Heroes take some concrete action to try to achieve their goals. It doesn't even need to be a big, overt action. In *Enough Said*, Eva (Julia Louis-Dreyfus) has not told her new boyfriend Albert (the late, great James Gandolfini) that she's also new best friends with Marianne (Catherine Keener). Marianne is perfect, except she keeps denigrating her ex-husband—Albert, which starts to impact Eva's relationship with him. When Albert discovers the deception, he breaks up with her.

> EVA
> I still really wanted us to keep seeing each other.

> ALBERT
> I wouldn't know how, you know?

> EVA
> I'm so so so sorry.

> ALBERT
> I know this sounds corny but you broke my heart. And I'm too old

```
for that shit. (sigh) And the worst
part, the worst part is you made me
look like an idiot in front of my
daughter.

            EVA
I'm the idiot. I'm the idiot.
```

This breakup is Eva's "All Is Lost" moment. In the last act, all Eva does is drive over to his house and park across the street and sit there. Albert sees her and comes out and they sit on the porch and talk. That's it. It's small, it's quiet, but it's perfect. Action is taken. And it has to be taken by Eva. Albert can't come up to her in a couple of weeks and say, "Let's go out again." Your protagonist has to be the one to take the action.

It doesn't matter if the action is successful. In *The Break-Up*, Vince Vaughn realizes that he has gone too far, that he has ruined the love of his life, and he goes and he makes the passionate speech to Jennifer Aniston to win her back. Does it work? No. They really break up. It happens. But at least he took the action. He tried to get her back, even though the effort failed.

CONFESSIONS, REVELATIONS, AND REALIZATIONS

Finally, revelations are complete and truths are told. This is the moment in *Tootsie* when Dustin Hoffman declares on a live broadcast that he is not, in fact, a woman, and in *The 40-Year-Old Virgin* when Steve Carell finally admits to Catherine Keener why he hasn't tried to go to bed with her. In the climactic moment of *Tropic Thunder*, while Kirk (Robert Downey Jr.) tries to convince Tugg (Ben Stiller) to escape the drug lords' camp, Kirk and Tugg's identity crises reach a new high (or low?) as all of Robert Downey Jr.'s masks dissolve.

```
            KIRK
Me? I know who I am! I'm a dude
playing a dude disguised as another
dude.
```

                    SANDUSKY (JAY BARUCHEL)
What?

          KIRK
You a dude that don't know what dude
he is!

          TUGG
Or are you a dude who has no idea
what dude he is and claims to know
what dude he is by playing other
dudes?

          KIRK
I know what dude I am!

          TUGG
You're scared.

          KIRK
I ain't scared. Scared of what?

          TUGG
Or scared of who?

          KIRK
Scared of who?

          SANDUSKY
Come on, guys. We really need to go!

          TUGG
     (whispers)
Scared of you.

          KIRK
     (looks at himself in mirror, and
     scared, smashes it, collapses on
     the floor)

          PORTNOY (JACK BLACK)
Jesus! What's going on?

                    TUGG
The dudes are emerging.

                    KIRK
          (slowly rising)
He's right, you know. I am not
Sergeant Lincoln Osiris.
          (pulls off Afro wig, revealing
          blonde hair)

                    ALPA CHINO (BRANDON T.
                    JACKSON)
We gotta roll out.

                    KIRK
          (Irish accent)
Nor am I Father O'Malley.
          (pulls off beard and mustache)
          (Southern accent)
Or Neil Armstrong.
          (takes out tinted contact lenses)
          (Australian accent)
I think I might be nobody.

                    SANDUSKY
          (beat)
Wow! The insecurity level
with you guys is ridiculous!

Whereas we might have thought that the scene was going to be
all about making Tugg remember who he is, instead the scene pulled
back the mask of Kirk, who's been compulsively playing other characters because at heart he doesn't know who he really is. Whether
serious or silly, en route to the climax, all disguises are taken off, all
deceptions ended, and all secrets are finally revealed.

REALIZATION OF AND RECOMMITMENT TO REVISED GOALS

After the Dark Night of the Soul, the mask is taken off for good,
backsliding is done and there's a renewed energy in achieving the
discovered goals. Tom (Joseph Gordon-Levitt) quits the greeting

card company and reinvests in his vision of becoming an architect (*(500) Days of Summer*); Annie (Kristen Wiig) starts baking again and restores her relationship with Lillian (Maya Rudolph) (*Bridesmaids*); and Michael Dorsey (Dustin Hoffman) finally helps to produce his roommate's play and begins to woo his true love, Julie (Jessica Lange), only this time as a man (*Tootsie*).

PERSONAL GROWTH ACCIDENTAL, INADVERTENT, OR UNHEROIC

It is true that in Race to the Finish, the Hero and the Comic Hero most nearly merge. As Vogler writes, "A Hero is someone who is willing to sacrifice his own needs on behalf of others. . . . At the root the idea of Hero is connected with self-sacrifice," and at this point in the story our dweebs, jerks, and idiots are more willing to risk their all for the people they love than at any other time in the narrative. But even though there is growth, the personal growth that happens is **accidental, inadvertent, or unheroic**. In *The 40-Year-Old Virgin*, Andy is heroically racing after Trish. However, since he doesn't know how to drive, he ends up racing after her on his bike (a bit less heroic) and finally catches up to her not because he put on a herculean burst of pedaling speed, but because he slams into a car, flies over the handlebars of the bike and crashes through both sides of a mobile billboard.

While one of the main points of the narrative is the transformation of the protagonist, and while your hero can now perform truly heroically when they need to, your Hero is merely transforming into a *better* person, not becoming a *perfect* person. Near the end of *Groundhog Day*, with Phil (Bill Murray) spends the day going around helping everyone in town. He changes the tires for an old lady, he saves the mayor's life by giving him the Heimlich maneuver, and gives away tickets to WrestleMania. His first chore of the day seems to be catching a little boy who every day falls from a tree.

```
EXT. RESIDENTIAL STREET — DAY

PHIL is walking briskly down the street, looks
at his watch, sees he's running late. Starts
running down the street, arms outstretched. In
```

a TREE a YOUNG BOY is playing on a limb, loses his balance. Just in time, PHIL catches him. As he catches the YOUNG BOY ...

> PHIL
>> What do you say?

As YOUNG BOY bounds out of PHIL's arms and runs away down the street

> PHIL

You little brat—you have never thanked me.
>> (Yelling after him)

I'll see you tomorrow ... maybe!

A more perfect person might say, "Wow! That was a close call! Are you okay? Be more careful in the future!" Except Phil is not perfect. He's human. He wants to be thanked! Even though he's evolved, he's still selfish enough to want to want some gratitude for being a nice guy and saving this kid each and every day.

As our characters become more actualized, they can never reach perfection, or even consistent, appropriate behavior. And the reason for this is the simple fact that no one is perfect. I'm not perfect, and neither is anyone who's reading this. Everyone you know is not perfect, so don't create characters who are better than you, or the people that you know.

SYMBOL OF GROWTH

In this section, a failure is rectified, a wrong is put to right, an obstacle is overcome—we see a concrete, tangible demonstration of our Hero's internal growth and transformation. Coop (Melissa McCarthy) steals the cool, spy-appropriate car in *Spy* to race to save Fine (Jude Law) and beat the bad guys. Annie (Kristen Wiig) at long last fixes her taillights in *Bridesmaids*. And Schmidt (Jonah Hill) and Jenko (Channing Tatum) finally recite the Miranda warning correctly when they arrest the perp (Rob Riggle) in *21 Jump Street*.

REVIEWING RACE TO THE FINISH

◀ Which character or event spurs your Comic Hero out of Disconnections?

◀ What action does your Hero take to achieve the final goal? Describe how your Hero and allies can overcome their obstacles in non-heroic fashion.

◀ What is finally revealed and/or realized at this point in the story?

◀ What symbolizes the growth of your Hero?

◀ In what way does the Hero's growth appear accidental, inadvertent, or unheroic?

* * *

So, with our Heroes stepping up and saving the day, with relationships rejoined and villains vanquished, there's just one more thing our Heroes have to attend to . . .

10.

"You Had Me at Hello"

RESTORATIONS AND CELEBRATIONS

"I intend to live forever—so far, so good."
—STEVEN WRIGHT

CELEBRATE GOOD TIMES . . . COME ON!

From the time of Aristophanes on down, comedies have typically
ended in celebrations of one kind or another. And what better way to
send off our Heroes than with a wedding (*Bridesmaids*, *The Hangover*,
The In-Laws) or at least, the wedding night, and the festivities that
follow (*40-Year-Old Virgin*)? Comedies have celebrated the good times
with dates or potential dates (*(500) Days of Summer*, *Enough Said*,
Adaptation), office parties (*21 Jump Street*, *9 to 5*), class parties (*Finding*

Nemo, An American in Paris), Christmas parties (*Elf, About a Boy*),
New Year's Eve parties (*When Harry Met Sally*), Groundhog Day Dance
parties (*Groundhog Day*), or just "let's get together and party" parties
(*Game Night, Girls Trip, This Is the End*). And there's no better party
than a rehearsal (*The Producers*), a performance (*The Full Monty*), a
premiere (*Bowfinger*), a convention (*Galaxy Quest*), or the Academy
Awards (*Tropic Thunder*)!

TRANSFORMATIONS AND THEMATIC RESOLUTIONS

Vogler, writing about the Road Back, states that "this stage marks the
decision to return to the ordinary world. The hero realizes that the
Special World must eventually be left behind." Campbell writes of the
"return and reintegration with society." But the comic hero doesn't
just return and reintegrate with society—the comic hero has been
transformed, and so it's a whole new person returning to a whole new
world, or at least the possibility of a whole new world.

In the Comic Hero's Journey, the experience has transformed the
comic hero, and there's a renewed energy in achieving discovered
goals. Tom (Joseph Gordon-Levitt) quits the greeting card company
and reinvests in his vision of becoming an architect (*(500) Days of
Summer*); Annie (Kristen Wiig) starts baking again and restores her
relationship with Lillian (Maya Rudolph) (*Bridesmaids*); and Michael
Dorsey (Dustin Hoffman) finally helps to produce his roommate's play
and begins to woo his true love, Julie, but this time as a man (*Tootsie*).

In *About a Boy*, Will Freeman (Hugh Grant) starts off as an immature man whose philosophy is the opposite of "No man is an island."
Quite to the contrary, he believes

```
                    WILL
     All men are islands. And what's
     more, this is the time to be one.
     This is an island age. A hundred
     years ago, for example, you had to
     depend on other people. No one had
     TV or CDs or DVDs or home espresso
     makers. As a matter of fact they
```

```
        didn't have anything cool. Whereas
        now you can make yourself a little
        island paradise. With the right
        supplies, and more importantly the
        right attitude, you can become sun-
        drenched, tropical, a magnet for
        young Swedish tourists.
```

But by the end of the film, Will and his whole outlook on life has been transformed. Surrounded by his girlfriend and his new extended family, he now says via voiceover:

```
                    WILL
        Every man is an island. But clearly
        some men are part of island chains.
        Below the surface, they are actually
        connected.
```

The transformations are always tied in to **thematic resolutions**. The plot may have been resolved in Race to the Finish, but the more important resolutions of theme are finalized here. In *Tootsie*, Michael Dorsey (Dustin Hoffman) is an arrogant, immature man who's inconsiderate of others. After his experience in dressing up as Dorothy, he's discovered a new perspective, and a new understanding of himself. In pleading his case to Julie (Jessica Lange), he says:

```
                  MICHAEL
        I just did it for the work. I didn't
        mean to hurt anybody.
        Especially you.

                   JULIE
        I miss Dorothy.

                  MICHAEL
        You don't have to. She's right here.
        And she misses you.
            (beat)
        Look, you don't know me from Adam.
        But I was a better man with you,
        as a woman than I ever was with a
```

```
woman,  as  a  man.  You  know  what  I
mean?

              JULIE
        (not  knowing  what  to  say)

              MICHAEL
I  just  gotta  learn  to  do  it
without  the  dress.
```

In the beginning of *Tootsie*, Michael Dorsey just want to prove that everyone's been wrong about him—that he is, indeed, a great actor. In the process, he discovers something more important to strive for and something more important about himself.

PROMISE OF A BETTER WORLD

Finally, there's the **promise of a better world**.

Onscreen title cards let us know how characters fare in the future in *Animal House* and *9 to 5*. In *Galaxy Quest*, the TV show within the movie is renewed after an 18-year hiatus. At the end of *Groundhog Day*, Bill Murray takes a look at the bucolic winter morning of Punxsutawney, Pennsylvania and turns to Andie MacDowell and says, "Let's live here." His transformation is complete and there's the promise of a simpler and happier life for the couple. The cast of actors in *Tropic Thunder* are last seen at the Oscars, in which Tugg (Ben Stiller) finally wins the Oscar, albeit for best documentary. We see the cast enjoying their triumph, including the rap star Alpa Chino (Brandon T. Jackson), who had been afraid to come out of the closet. Now we see him beaming to the world as he shares an on-camera kiss with Lance Bass. It's the promise, if not the fact, of a better world.

And you don't have to have a Hollywood-style happy ending, you don't have to *show* me the better world, you don't have to take me to the wedding, but you at least have to hold out the hope for one. For example, *The Break-Up* was a rom-com that consciously subverted the form. Usually in a romcom, the protagonist has a heartfelt speech which wins the heart of the girl at the end. But in this case, Vince Vaughn gives the heartfelt speech and the girl, Jennifer Aniston, says, in effect, "Forget it." That ship has sailed on their relationship, and despite Vaughan's impassioned speech, their break-up is now permanent. In the original last scene, Vaughan and Aniston run into each other at an art fair, and the joke was that each was with a date that totally resembled their former beau—Aniston's date was the spitting image of Vaughan, and Vaughan's date was a dead ringer for Aniston. There's some awkward chatter, an insincere promise to get together, and then the two couples part forever.

But this ending tested very poorly with the audience, I'm guessing because they substituted a joke for a satisfying resolution. So they reshot the closing scenes so that Aniston and Vaughan are alone, walking down a street. They meet each other and for a moment, they just connect. There's a little enigmatic nod and a smile. That's it. No big reunion. No wild make-up kiss. But that was enough to satisfy the next test audience, because it at least *promised* a more hopeful world.

Joseph Campbell wrote that "The happy ending is justly scorned as a misrepresentation; for the world, as we know it, as we have seen it, yields but one ending: death, disintegration, and . . . the passing of the forms that we have loved. . . . But the happy ending of the fairy tale, the myth, and the divine comedy of the soul, is to be read, not as a contradiction, but as a transcendence of the universal tragedy of man." For example, Danny Rubin's original ending of *Groundhog Day* revealed that "Rita, Phil's producer and love interest, was trapped in her own endless repetition, and that there was no existential relief in sight," as Tad Friend wrote in his *New Yorker* profile of Harold Ramis. But Ramis knew from experience that this sort of "cosmic irony" left audiences unfulfilled and dissatisfied. Your characters can fail, but you still need to provide, even in some small way, a "transcendence of the universal tragedy of man."

At the end of Charlie Kaufman's *Adaptation*, Charlie (Nicolas Cage) finally gets the courage to kiss his former girlfriend Amelia and tell her that he loves her. She responds by telling him she's already with somebody and starts to walk away before turning, and saying, "I love you, too," smiles and then walks away. As Charlie drives away we hear in voiceover:

```
        CHARLIE V.O.
So, Kaufman drives off from his
encounter with Amelia filled for the
first time with hope. I like this.
This is good.
```

THE COMIC PARADIGM

So what we have here is a kind of **comic paradigm**. Our heroes are bumbling along, often blissfully unaware of their predicament and limitations. Then some agency, some cosmic force disrupts the normal life, and pushes that person off balance. Our heroes first desperately try to return to what they thought was "the Normal World": a world that was working for them. But through the events of the narrative, our heroes discover a new normal, a better way of standing in the world. So that even if your character is "unsuccessful," like Julia Roberts at the end of *My Best Friend's Wedding*, our heroes have found a way to make the world a better fit for them.

AND SO IT GOES . . .

My friend, the playwright, teacher, and performer Deb Margolin, has written, "All plays are about love; all plays are about death! Comedy just always shows what absurd and tragic bedfellows these make! The alembic of comedy makes investigations of the most difficult and disgusting aspects of being human—of being an immortal spirit in a mortal body, of losing those you love to death or indifference, of failing, of flailing, of being the asses that we all are—digestible, manageable, and sometimes radically pleasant!"

If there's one thought I want to leave you with, it's that character has to take precedence over plot and over jokes. Funny is subjective. If you chase after funny, what's funny to one person might not be funny to another, But humans . . . and what makes humans so absurd and so infuriating, and so surprising, that's something we all share. We're all human, so we have that going for us, at least. So, write that. Premise, character, and see what happens. Write the truth about humans. And if you write the truth, it just might be funny. And if it's not, at least it's the truth.

REVIEWING RESTORATIONS AND CELEBRATIONS

◀ How is your Hero's transformation dramatized?

◀ How have you resolved the thematic questions of your story?

◀ How have you shown the Promise of a Better World?

◀ Create a unique celebration to dramatize the narrative and thematic conclusion to your story.

11.

"Why a Duck?"

Q & A

"What's another word for thesaurus?"
—Steven Wright

Where Should This Happen in the Movie?
When should the break-up in a romcom occur?
How long should Act 1 be before the inciting incident?
When should the Object of Desire be introduced into the story?

There are probably great answers to these, but unfortunately, these are in many ways the wrong questions. Structure is a form, but it needn't be a box. It's not something that you have to do. *This* doesn't have to happen at page 52. You don't have to do *that* at the 75% mark.

All of the stages in the Comic Hero's Journey happen in most movies, but not at set page numbers or percentage points. These are stations of the cross that may happen at different points or in different sequences in different narratives. So yes, many scripts have the dark night of the soul moment about two-thirds, three-quarters of the way through the script. But it's not a rule, not obligatory. What's necessary is following your characters through their story and telling their story authentically and honestly.

What's the definition of *mensch*?
Mensch is a Yiddish word that means . . . mensch.[1]

I'm graduating with my screenwriting MFA and the plan is to move to LA. Besides a car, what do you recommend packing in my LA starter kit? Tangible or intangible answers okay.
First off, preliminary congratulations!

Here's what I'd try to include in your starter kit:

A job—While you're waiting to open your film at Sundance, you've got to survive. Now, if you've got a trust fund from Zuckerberg, congrats! If not, you need to figure out a way to keep yourself sane, safe, and solvent while writing the Great American Screenplay. When you're broke, you're desperate, and LA can smell desperate a mile away (as will all possible romantic partners). Make sure you have a plan to keep you going for as long as it takes. Remember, it takes most people years to become overnight successes. And the housing here ain't cheap.

Your contact list—Your jobs and opportunities will come from people who know you, so start with the people who you already know. When you hit LA, make a list of everyone in LA you've ever met, or your parents had met or who dated a cousin or who you served a latte to while waiting tables. You never know where or when the next job or project will come from. In the same vein, practice this mantra:

Say yes to the universe. Go to that party, or event, or play or art opening. Yes, you're tired from fighting traffic, but again, you never know who you'll connect with, or reconnect with or what new project you'll become involved with. Around the corner may be the next

---

[1] *Mensch* is a Yiddish word that means mensch, a good man, a good person.

love of your life, or your next boss, or that friend from high school who you lost touch with. So just say yes. (Just note—this is not networking in the negative sense that networking is just making use of people for your own ends. This is opening yourself up to people and possibilities. This is building your support team.)

A sense of humor—you're going to need it.

Hand sanitizer—Ditto.

Flexibility—Yes, you're on your path, but sometimes the path bends or turns. A friend of mine was a TV executive waiting to run her own studio. Then she wasn't, because she was let go. She managed to change course, and now she's one of the top script consultants in the business. Another friend wrote a screenplay that he couldn't find a buyer for; so he turned it into a novel that got bought, published, and was optioned . . . wait for it . . . to be adapted as a screenplay. Be ready to adapt, yourself.

Oh, and a pair of shorts and a T-shirt—the weather is usually lovely! Welcome to LA!

What are your Top 10 American comedies?

Sometimes at the end of one of my workshops or seminars, I'm asked, "What's your favorite comedy?" I find that an almost impossible question to answer. How can I select just one? I love comedy, I love comedians, I love great writing—there are literally dozens I can watch and enjoy over and over again.

So I don't bother saying, "This one's my favorite," or "This one's the funniest." Because like potato chips, you can't pick just one. Or even ten. But I can think of a list of great comic artists and ask myself, "Which one's the best *Road* movie, or best Woody Allen, or best Python?" And so here's my list of "IF YOU CAN ONLY SEE ONE _____ MOVIE, THE ONE YOU SHOULD SEE IS____!"

These might not even be the funniest, but they are the ones which I think most epitomize what's greatest in comedy writing, performance, and filmmaking. (Some of you might notice that I still have more than ten. What can I say? Math was never my strong suit.)

In no particular order:

Groundhog Day. A delicious premise, great supporting cast, and the best Bill Murray performance until *St. Vincent*. And let's not forget about the late, great Harold Ramis's brave direction. He helped give the movie heart, and when he refused to cut the "Old Man Dying" sequence, gave it soul as well.

The Grand Budapest Hotel. Some people feel that Wes Anderson is an acquired taste. Well, acquire it, already! This stylish, deceptively thoughtful confection features a star-studded panoply of great comic performances: Ralph Fiennes, Harvey Keitel, Adrien Brody, Willem Dafoe, Edward Norton, Jeff Goldblum. What starts as a light, delicious fairy tale evolves into an intricate, multilayered, bittersweet romance of love lost and found and a world found and lost. And the best score of the year.

Sleeper / Annie Hall / Manhattan. Okay, I understand the contro-versy, but if I'm being honest, these films helped shape my comedy education. Sorry. As it is, I couldn't narrow it down to just one Woody Allen, but these three stand out above all the rest. *Annie Hall* and *Manhattan* broke new ground and often broke our hearts, while *Sleeper* just split our sides. Classic moment: Woody and the giant bag of cocaine.

Bowfinger. Yes, *Bowfinger*. Maybe not as funny as *The Jerk* or as romantic as *L.A. Story* or *Roxanne*, but in its own way it was the ulti-mate romantic comedy: a daffy valentine to actors, writers, directors, producers, and anyone who ever aspired to any of those roles. That being said, an Honorable Mention has to go to *Waiting for Guffman*.

The Producers. Forget the film of the musical. This is prime, rude, and funny Mel Brooks, with a pitch-perfect performance by Gene Wilder and the gargantuan talent of the late, great Zero Mostel. Best moment: as the chorus belts out "Springtime for Hitler," the camera pans an audience full of slack-jawed New Yorkers, frozen in horror and disbelief.

Road to Utopia. Who doesn't love Bob and Bing and the *Road* movies? Utopia finds our boys in Alaska and is full talking bears, talking fish, and the best sight gags, ad-libs, and asides of the series. That sound you hear is the fourth wall being constantly broken, as our lovable rogues seem to talk to us more than they do the other characters.

Modern Times. Charlie and the Age of Industry, as he is literally swallowed by the assembly line and spit out, a bit worse for wear but still full of pluck and hope.

There's Something About Mary. The Farrelly Brothers' best. In this film, they navigate the line of gross-out humor and bad taste without crossing over (much). Most memorable scene: some say it's Cameron

Diaz's hair "gel," but I vote for Ben Stiller in braces, zipping up while the "frank and beans" are still out. In a bathroom that begins to echo the famous Marx Brothers stateroom scene, the Farrellys reached comic heights as most men in the audience reach for their . . . uh . . . And you might say that this film led to . . .

The 40-Year-Old Virgin. Judd Apatow's brilliant melding of raunchy humor with heartfelt character comedy. And the film works because we're always made to care for Steve Carell's arrested adolescent adult, as opposed to simply mocking him. And when he and Catherine Keener finally do the deed, what more perfect ending could there be then the entire cast singing and dancing to "Aquarius!"

Okay, so that's eleven, but already I'm despondent over the exclusion of James Brooks's masterful, funny, and touching *Broadcast News*; Ben Stiller's acid love letter to the film industry, *Tropic Thunder*; Danny Kaye's *The Court Jester* (Kaye: "But did you put the pellet with the poison in the vessel with the pestle?" Mildred Natwick: "No! The pellet with the poison's in the flagon with the dragon! The vessel with the pestle has the brew that is true!"); Hugh Grant in the best romantic comedy between a grown man and a boy, *About a Boy*. . . .

And talking about romantic comedies, how the hell could I forget to include *When Harry Met Sally*? Or *Big*? Or *Tootsie*?

What are your Top 10 British comedies?

When I'm in the U.K., I'm often asked, "What's your favorite British comedy?" Again, it's impossible to narrow it down to just one. Favorite contemporary comedy? Favorite Ealing comedy? Favorite Python? There is no favorite, because these are some damn funny apples and oranges.

I can still make a list, however—of my favorite artists, writers, and performers, and pick which one of their films I most enjoy. So here's my list of my favorite British comedies. These might not make your list as the favorite, or even what you think are the funniest (remember that funny is subjective) but they're the ones which I think most epitomize what's greatest in comedy writing, performance, and filmmaking.

Favorite Peter Sellers Movie

Dr. Strangelove. A pitch-black satire that promised to help us "stop worrying and love the Bomb. In a film abounding with great performances (George C. Scott as a general eager to make love *or* war, Sterling Hayden as a man willing to go to any lengths to protect his

Precious Bodily Fluids), Peter Sellers tops them all with his portrayal of the fastidious RAF officer Lionel Mandrake, the slightly overwhelmed President of the United States Merkin Muffley and the eponymous Dr. Strangelove, a maniacal ex-Nazi scientist who has figured out how to make the Armageddon as enjoyable as possible. Favorite Moment: Slim Pickens, riding the bomb down to oblivion as he waves his cowboy hat and "wa-hoos" his way to oblivion. The film was originally financed with the understanding that Sellers would play four parts, including Major T.J. "King" Kong, but Sellers sprained an ankle, and was unable to film in the cramped bomber set, so he was replaced by veteran western actor Pickens. My wife's Favorite Moment? Dr. Strangelove trying not to "Heil."

Favorite British Comedy About Shakespeare

Shakespeare in Love. This period charmer, co-written by Marc Norman and Tom Stoppard (I guess this is also my favorite Stoppard movie), *Shakespeare in Love* is a witty and passionate wet kiss to the theater and features one of the truly delicious turns by Geoffrey Rush as an unscrupulous yet goodhearted producer, Philip Henslowe. (He must be a distant ancestor of Zero Mostel's Max Bialystock from *The Producers*.) Favorite Moment: Shakespeare, watching aghast as a stuttering actor prepares to open the play. In agony, he turns to Henslowe, "We are lost!" Henslowe replies, "No, it will turn out well." "How will it?" Will demands. Henslowe simply replies, "I don't know, it's a mystery." All those who work in the arts know the feeling that nothing will work out, and yet, often it does. How? It's a mystery.

Favorite Nick Hornby / Hugh Grant Comedy

About a Boy. More than a bromance, *About a Boy* is a romcom without a rom, but one with more heart and soul than most other romantic comedies that are featuring age and gender-appropriate partners. And maybe now we can put to rest the old saw that says that voiceover narration is hacky or a crutch. Hugh Grant's voiceover in this film conveys character, tone, theme, and delivers the best of Nick Hornby's prose.

Favorite *Wallace and Gromit* comedy not about Wallace and Gromit

Chicken Run. Yes, *Chicken Run*. Maybe not as classic as a Wallace and Gromit short, but where else can you find the poultry version of *The Great Escape, Stalag 17*, and *Prison Break* all rolled up into one? Favorite

151

supporting chicken: The delightful Babs, a permanently befuddled chicken constantly knitting her way from calamity to another.

Second Favorite Non-Python Python Movie

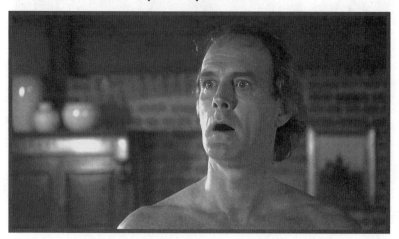

A Fish Called Wanda. Yes, there's Michael Palin and an insanely inspired Kevin Kline, but the beating, passionate heart of this film is John Cleese in his best acting job since . . . ever. It was directed by the then 80-year-old Charles Crichton, who had helmed such classics as of British cinema as *Dead of Night* and *The Lavender Hill Mob*. "On the first day of shooting, Cleese gave Crichton a T-shirt that said 'Age and Treachery Will Always Overcome Youth and Skill.'" Favorite speech: Cleese as Archie Leach (Cary Grant's real name) is trying to explain to Wanda why being with her makes him feel free. "Wanda, do you have any idea what it's like being English? Being so correct all the time, being so stifled by this dread of, of doing the wrong thing, of saying to someone, "Are you married?" and hearing, "My wife left me this morning," or saying, uh, "Do you have children?" and being told they all burned to death on Wednesday. You see, Wanda, we'll all terrified of embarrassment. That's why we're so . . . dead. Most of my friends are dead, you know, we have these piles of corpses to dinner. But you're alive, God bless you, and I want to be, I'm so fed up with all this. I want to make love with you, Wanda. I'm a good lover—at least, used to be, back in the early 14th century. Can we go to bed?"

Favorite Non-Python Python Movie

Brazil. Is it even a comedy? Is it even British? It's my list, and I say, "Yes!" and I say it's Terry Gilliam's mess of a masterpiece. Studio exec Sid Sheinberg obviously agreed that it was a mess, and since the film was a few minutes over the contracted length, had it recut to eliminate the complex, dark ending that incorporated the tag line: "Love Conquers All." Sheinberg was determined to release the film with the "Love Conquers All" cut, but Gilliam was able to hold several illegal private screenings in LA, including screening the film for the LA Film Critics Association "who promptly voted it Best Picture, Best Screenplay, and Best Director, even though it hadn't been released." End result? Masterpiece won out over mess, and Gilliam's cut was eventually released. Favorite Moment: Robert De Niro first appearance as the gun-wielding, SWAT team–attired heating engineer Harry Tuttle.

Favorite Our-Economy's-in-the-Shitter Comedy

The Full Monty. OK, Six guys take their clothes off, but more than that, the movie explores the social disruption of the Thatcher years and finds hope in a bunch of working class blokes exposing all to regain purpose and camaraderie in their lives. Favorite Moment: Dancing in the unemployment line to "Hot Stuff."

Favorite Simon Pegg Comedy

Hot Fuzz. Which also makes it my favorite Edgar Wright (director) and Nick Frost (costar) movie as well! Better than parody, *Hot Fuzz* is a loving, if loopy, tribute not only to those buddy-cop action pics starring Gibson, Willis, or Schwarzenegger, but also to the bucolic English villages that harbor the quaint, eccentric British characters. Favorite Moment: High noon shootout on High Street.

Favorite Terrorism Comedy

***Four Lions* (2010)**. You can't make a comedy about a bunch of terror-
ists out to blow up London, can you? Well maybe you can't, but Chris
Morris's apocalyptic satire finds the humanity in the inhuman actions
of a bunch of inept would-be suicide bombers. Despite yourself, you
find yourself empathizing and rooting for our heroes to somehow
get out of their own way and to, well, not blow us, or themselves, up.

Favorite Python Movie
Monty Python and the Life of Brian. More than a series of sketches,
Brian is a brilliant, complete film, with a coda that captures in a song
the entire meaning of comedy and meaning of life. Favorite Moment:
The whole film, from the wise men barging into the wrong stable
through to Eric Idle singing:

> For life is quite absurd
> And death's the final word
> You must always face the curtain with a bow.
> Forget about your sin—give the audience a grin
> Enjoy it—it's your last chance anyhow.[2]

---

[2] Copyright © 1979 KAY-GEE-BEE MUSIC LTD. and EMI VIRGIN MUSIC LTD.

So that's my list. You probably have a completely different list of ten. And you know what? You're right too. As a Yank, I'm probably overlooking some gem that might not have translated so well on my side of the pond, just means that I have some gems I can look forward to discovering! So let's watch 'em all!

Do I have to write a screenplay that's modeled on the Comic Hero's Journey?

Fuck no! If you have a great movie that doesn't fit any pattern, the hell with everyone else, just write it. And if it's great, it'll be great.

But there's a reason that these patterns occur and reoccur, because they're time-tested storytelling techniques. If you don't follow them, that's great, but that might be one reason why a screenplay isn't working. If you want to invent a car that doesn't have an internal combustion engine, more power to you. But if you invent a car in which hamsters are on a treadmill and it's not working, take a look at the engine. That might be the case. (Except if you have active enough hamsters—then it just might work.

I'm currently writing a comedy ensemble road movie. I wanted to ask how you would outline the story before we begin writing the screenplay.

Well, there's a couple ways. You can write out a detailed outline of the film. Some people prefer to write out 60 index cards, each representing one of the 60 beats in the movie. Unless you really enjoy outlining, I would suggest that you write a treatment as though it was a short story, because if you were to tell this story to someone over a couple of beers or a cup of coffee, you would tell it as a story. It starts out with these characters, then this happens, which leads to this, and so on. If the story works for you, later you can worry about structuring it into sequences, scenes and acts. But whatever method you choose, the one that's best is the one that helps you take it from concept to completed pages. (And keep your treatment short. Michael Hauge recommends no more than three to five pages.)

Can the Comic Heroes become heroic in the last act?

Yes, but remember they're still not perfect, and it's a mistake if you transform them from something flawed to something flawless. None of us are flawless. If you give them skills, they become more heroic. They become more romantic. And, yes, Phil Connors in *Groundhog Day* is a much better person by the end of the film than at the beginning. But he's still a smartass, he's still a wisecracker, and he's still selfish and human enough to want to be thanked by the kid in the tree.

Do these concepts translate to television writing?

Not so much. Television writing has a different structure in terms of basic setup and ongoing relationships. Into those relationships you toss a problem, and as you see how the ripples of the problem spread out, they quickly—and by quickly, I mean within 22 minutes—are dissolved and reintegrated back into the initial situation. A film features a problem that can be solved (or not) within two hours. In a sitcom, there's an ongoing dilemma that can never be solved, because it's the basic premise of the series. In the structure of a sitcom there is no Normal World because every episode is already engaged with the series dilemma. In *Everybody Loves Raymond*, the titular character's parents live next door and they keep on bumping into his life. That's the dilemma. If they solve that, by moving away, you've completely changed the series. Within the dilemma, every episode features a further complication that will need to be addressed. For instance, maybe this year Debra decides that Marie and Frank will not be in the family Christmas photo. (That's going to cause some problems, no?) While there are similarities, for the most part, sitcom structure has its own unique structure.

Cary Grant in *Arsenic and Old Lace* is a perfectly normal character surrounded by very flawed characters. Are there more such examples? Or is it best to use a flawed protagonist?
Cary Grant may seem normal, but he's not, because a normal guy wouldn't be so concerned that he's going insane, just like the rest of his insane family. When it turns out that he was adopted, he feels much better. But throughout the film, he's frantically attempting to cope, trying his best to keep one crazy person away from another crazy person, often unsuccessfully. He's constantly flummoxed and confused. So I would say that he's not a perfectly normal character. Yes, compared to many of the characters in *Arsenic and Old Lace*, he's more normal than they are, but he's still what we would call a Non-Hero— he lacks many of the skills needed to deal with this situation. Action heroes may be upset or depressed, but they're rarely flummoxed and confused. They see the problem, and they do their best to solve the problem. Sometimes they're physically unable to solve problems, but not through any lack of will or skill. In a comedy, characters lack basic wills and skills. And so even a character, a "straight" character like Cary Grant in *Arsenic and Old Lace*, is still not "perfectly normal."

In a romantic comedy is it mandatory to have a literal race to the finish? My third act primarily deals with the protagonist's personal growth, so I don't have a literal race to the finish.
As I've mentioned earlier, one of my favorite comedies from recent years was *Enough Said* with James Gandolfini and Julia Louis-Dreyfus.

At the end she drives by his house, as she's done before, and she waits outside his house. And he shows up, and she opens her door and she goes and starts to have a conversation with him. So race is metaphorical. There isn't a race per se at the end of *Groundhog Day* where Bill Murray's action is simply to do all the things to help people, which helps get him through his day. He'll do the same thing tomorrow, because he's accepted his fate. So it doesn't need to be a literal race, but there does need to be some kind of an effort on the part of your character to resolve the problem. As long as your protagonist takes action to affect his or her personal growth, that may be enough.

There are a lot of comedies out there that just don't work, *Sex Tape* being a current example. What are the main reasons a comedy will not work out?
There's a lot of reasons comedies don't work, but the main ones usually are some combination of not trusting the characters, condescending to the characters or to the audience, trying to make things funnier (or raunchier or more shocking) than they are or need to be, and/or trying to catch a cultural wave that might have been cresting when the project started, but now three or five or seven years later when the film has finally come out, discovering that the wave, the culture, and the potential audience has moved on.

Do all movies have a three-act structure?
Some do, maybe even most. But I don't think that you want to apply the same structure to every movie. And if you find a different way to tell your story, you find a different structure to tell your story. *Groundhog Day*, for instance, has a seven-act structure, which is unusual. It has a long set-up, and then it follows the five stages of grief by Kubler-Ross. It goes through **denial**; a very short **anger** section; **negotiation**—that's where he's trying to make it work for him, going to sleep with all the girls; **depression**; and then there's a long **acceptance** sequence. And the acceptance sequence is actually divided into three sections. First, where he simply accepts it, and he finally figures out how to get Andie MacDowell to believe him. Then, there's the "old man" sequence, where

the old man dies and he tries to stop it. The studio wanted them to cut that sequence out; they thought it was kind of a bummer—this was supposed to be a big, fun, summertime comedy. Luckily, the filmmakers fought that battle and won because the old man dying was thematically important. Even though Phil was in some ways immortal, it was important to let him know that he wasn't a god, that he didn't have the power of life over death. And finally, there's the last part of the acceptance where it's the Groundhog Day Dance and then the next morning.

Structure should help you tell the stories you want to tell, not prevent you from telling your unique story in your unique way.

Is Sleepless in Seattle *a comedy?*

Sleepless in Seattle? Okay, that's a good question, so here's my personal opinion. A comedy is not determined by the number of laughs in it. A comedy's determined by the point of view of the characters and the point of view of the filmmakers. So, yes. A comedy starts with a comic premise, an impossibility or improbability that could never or probably would never happen, but if it did happen, what would happen then? How likely is it that some nine-year-old is going to call up to a radio show and have somebody in Seattle get to somebody in Baltimore and have them meet at the Empire State Building at midnight? That's an improbability. But if it DID happen, what would happen then?

So yes, *Sleepless in Seattle*, although based on a drama, is in my estimation a romantic comedy. One way you can see that it's a comedy is look at your mirror characters. That's a term that Michael Hauge uses, the mirror characters, the reflection, your best friend, your buddy, the people you talk to. Rosie O'Donnell is the female friend, and the male friend is Rob Reiner. So your mirror characters are definitely comic characters. They're not there to deepen the drama. This is not *An Affair to Remember*. Watch *Affair to Remember*, watch *Sleepless in Seattle*, see which one makes you laugh more.

How do you make an annoying character likeable?

The problem is with the term "likeable." Not everybody can be likeable. Not everybody *is* likeable. The important thing is that they're relatable.

Can I relate to them? Do I understand them? Is there another charac-
ter who understands them, or has some sort of empathy for them? As
Ricky Gervais has said, "I can't laugh at someone I don't like, either.
The most important thing in comedy for me is empathy. Laurel and
Hardy got it right a hundred years ago. It's the relationship that reso-
nates with me."

I outline everything—what's wrong with that?
There's nothing wrong with that. But the danger in outlining is that
as you're developing the story from the perspective of plot, you may
be ignoring the developmental possibilities from the perspective of
the characters. When you start to follow the story from the characters' point of view, maybe they don't do what you thought they were
going to. The point is that premise does not determine development
or outcome. Your characters determine development, springing from
the premise, guided by theme. Just because A happens doesn't mean
B happens. Your premise has got to leave enough open room for your
characters to breathe.

Let's say *Wedding Crashers* was never made, and I secretly gave you
the premise of these two guys who crash weddings, and one of them
meets this special girl. If I give the premise to twenty people, you
could have twenty different movie, because all twenty would develop
the movie in different ways, given what your theme is and what you
want to talk about.

Even though these twenty movies share many of the same struc-
tural elements, what differentiates them is theme. Different themes
bring on different characters, and those different characters create
different lines of action.

In writing, the question is, *what are you talking about?* And that
ultimately is a form of self-confession—how you see the world, what
you value, what's important to you. You're always writing about yourself, from your own point of view, your own sense of what the world
is and what the world should be. And writing a screenplay is a way
of sharing that.

Do you have any suggestions about writing a horror comedy or comedy horror?

If you take a glance at some recent offerings, like *Shaun of the Dead*, *Scream*, or *Zombieland*, what you'll notice right away is that the filmmakers have put decidedly un-heroic characters in decidedly terrifying situations. So, in whatever horrific premise you can think up, make sure that several main characters would do just as well if they were in a Judd Apatow movie. Just think of the cast of *Silicon Valley* battling zombies, vampires, or triffids—see, you've got a good start to a horror-comedy mash-up right there.

I would like some advice with regards to a script I am currently writing. This probably applies to any genre but in my opinion, certainly comedy. I have a character who uses slang expressions in his language but I'm not entirely sure whether or not I should be using the correct language for the purpose of the script. When I watch comedies such as anything by Seth Rogen or Judd Apatow, I wonder if the dialogue used is written prior to production or if most of it is improv. Do you have any tips/tricks that could make this easier to notice?

You seem to be asking a number of related questions

1. Yes, if you're character uses slang, then that's the dialogue you should be writing for him/her. As for spelling, there's some latitude there, although some forms are already well established, For instance, if your character is an old hipster, you should have him say, "Gimme five, man" as opposed to, "Give me five, man."

2. In an Apatow or Rogen movie, there's a script that they'll follow, but then there'll be numerous takes where they'll improvise lines over and over, using the best ones for the final cut. For example, this scene from *Knocked Up*: youtube.com/watch?v=AOVehIKpm4k

3. Best way to figure out if you're writing dialogue, or just misspelling all over the place, start reading screenplays of movies that contain similar characters (or at least characters who speak somewhat similar to how you imagine your characters speaking) to see how those experienced writers handled the same problem.

I'm a recent Ivy League graduate that just finished a screenplay about a gifted teen hoping to survive his last year of high school. I thought you might be able to offer guidance on my next steps. Any help would be greatly appreciated!

OK, next step is to do a reading of it. You don't need to get and rehearse a cast of professional actors—just gather a bunch of intelligent friends to read the parts, an equal bunch of friends to listen, provide wine and cheese and make sure to record the entire session. Have someone else besides you read the stage directions. The most important prep work you should do is highlighting in everybody's script exactly which stage directions are read—don't read every single last one, or your audience will die of boredom before the end of Act 2. You can ask for feedback, but don't ask for suggestions—let them write their own screenplay. You only want to know six things: Where was it confusing? Where was it boring? What parts were exciting? What characters did you like? What did you want more of? What did you want less of?

If you're simply looking to break into the business, some of my friends have written terrific books on the subject: *Hollywood Game Plan* by Carole Kirschner and *The Script-Selling Game* by Kathie Fong Yoneda, to name two.

How can a character be funny in a tragic plot?

Even if the plot is tragic, you can find comedy by introducing comic characters who are peripheral to the tragedy, and therefore free to pursue comic behavior and action. For example, *Manchester by the Sea* is acknowledged to be a very serious movie, but the role of the teenager is not totally serious, as he navigates between the death of his father (tragic) and trying to get one of the two girls he's dating to go all the way (comic).

Another method is to allow the main character to have moments of bewilderment and bafflement. Even though he or she may be experiencing tragedy, those human moments can add lightness to an otherwise dark story.

I'm just starting out and finding it difficult to find how to communicate my idea of comedy through screenwriting. Any ideas on how to start?

If you were an aspiring painter, you would be told to copy the masters as a way of working on technique, as well as finding your own visual expression.

My advice would be somewhat the same. Watch movies that you love, and then watch them again to see how they're constructed, and then read the screenplays of those movies. If there are multiple drafts prior to the shooting draft that you can get your hands on, all the better.

Write a scene imitating the voice, tone, and style. Then write a short screenplay (20 pages or less). Then another. Organize a reading of that short screenplay, to hear how your voice is developing. Once you get to a point where you like what you hear, apply it to a full-length screenplay.

Don't worry that you're, in part, copying the masters. Tarantino is acclaimed as an original writer, but even he would admit that he's a master aggregator of past masters.

I've heard about pitch-fests. Is it easy to sell pitches there? Or should I just send one to a company?

Very few companies accept unsolicited material, and it's very rare to sell an original spec script. Pitch fests are places in which you should look to make a connection, and by a connection, I mean you might be able to have a conversation with a professional in the film industry. They are usually not looking to hire you or buy your script. Instead, you should see it as a learning opportunity for yourself.

Your focus should be to try to study in a film program or get involved in the film industry in your own region and get some experience. After you get more experience, you can try to get people to read your work by entering script contests and applying for fellowships and programs, but realize that the competition is very, very fierce.

One resource that you should take advantage of is Scriptchat. com—it's an online community of writers and filmmakers from around the world.

I'm sorry to say that only the most experienced and highly sought-out writers are able to sell a pitch. It seems like you think that there's a lucrative market for an idea. Unfortunately, that's not the case. For new writers, only a completed script would be able to be sold—there is no shortcut or easy way. Even then, only a small proportion of finished scripts are sold. Most new writers use their scripts as writing samples, and simply hope that their completed script will lead to a job.

I'd suggest focusing less on making a quick sale, and focusing more on improving your writing.

In general, online pitch meetings with strangers is useful for practice, but rarely, if ever, results in a sale. But if you do it with the thought of practicing pitching, and perhaps connecting with someone in the industry, it might be worth it.

I recently read a comedy thriller (defined so by the author) wherein the main character dies at the end. As far as I recall, that is a tragedy, not a comedy. However, does it qualify as a comedy if the character changes before he dies, or does a comedy by definition end happily with a wedding?
In comic films or plays, main characters can die, either ironically or, shifting the mood, tragically. A tragic death or event is often found in tragi-comedies or comedy-dramas. It's rare that it would involve the death of a main character, but it does happen. Woody Allen dies (but comes back as a ghost) at the end of *Love and Death*, and William Holden ironically narrates his own murder in *Sunset Boulevard*.

* * *

Do you have a question about comedy? Please feel free to send it to me at Steve@KaplanComedy.com.

About the Author

Steve Kaplan is one of the industry's most respected and sought-after experts on comedy, and author of the best-selling book, *The Hidden Tools of Comedy: The Serious Business of Being Funny*. The artists he's taught, directed, or produced have won Oscars, Emmys, Golden Globes, and WGA awards. In addition to having taught at UCLA, NYU, and Yale, Steve created the HBO Workspace and the HBO New Writers Program. He has served as a consultant and/or taught workshops at companies as DreamWorks, Disney, Aardman Animations, HBO, and others.

In New York, Steve was cofounder and artistic director of Manhattan Punch Line Theatre, where he developed such writers as Peter Tolan (*Analyze This, Finding Amanda*), writer and producer David Crane (*Friends, Joey, The Class*), Steve Skrovan (*Everybody Loves Raymond*), Michael Patrick King (*2 Broke Girls, Sex and the City*), Howard Korder (*Boardwalk Empire*), writer/producer Tracy Poust (*Ugly Betty, Will & Grace*), David Ives (*All in the Timing, Venus in Fur*), and Mark O'Donnell (*Hairspray*), and introduced such performers as Lewis Black, Nathan Lane, John Leguizamo, Mercedes Ruehl, and Oliver Platt.

In Los Angeles, he created the HBO New Writers Project, discovering HBO Pictures screenwriter Will Scheffer (*Big Love, Getting On*) and performer/writer Sandra Tsing Loh; and the HBO Workspace, a developmental workshop in Hollywood that introduced and/or presented performers such as Jack Black and Tenacious D, Kathy Griffin, Bob Odenkirk and David Cross (*Mr. Show*), and stand-up comic Paul F. Tompkins. At the Workspace, he was executive producer for the award-winning HBO Original Programming documentary *Drop Dead Gorgeous*. Steve has directed in regional theaters and Off-Broadway (including Sandra Tsing Loh's *Aliens in America* at Second Stage).

In addition to private coaching and one-on-one consultations, Steve has taught his Comedy Intensive workshops to thousands of students in the United States and countries around the world, including London, Toronto, Galway, Athens, Paris, Tel Aviv, Sydney, Melbourne, Rio, Munich, New Zealand, and Singapore. This year, he will be presenting seminars and workshops in Los Angeles, San Francisco, Milan, New York, London, and via Skype, Sweden.

He lives happily in Chatsworth, California, with his beautiful and talented wife Kathrin King Segal and their three cats. www.KaplanComedy.com Steve@KaplanComedy.com

THE HIDDEN TOOLS OF COMEDY
THE SERIOUS BUSINESS OF BEING FUNNY

STEVE KAPLAN

While other books give you tips on how to "write funny," this book offers a paradigm shift in understanding the mechanics and art of comedy, and the proven, practical tools that help writers translate that understanding into successful, commercial scripts. *The Hidden Tools of Comedy* unlocks the unique secrets and techniques of writing comedy. Kaplan deconstructs sequences in popular films and TV that work and don't work, and explains what tools were used (or should have been used).

"Fresh insights with a 'why didn't I think of that' on every page. Steve Kaplan is a true comedy maven. Don't know what that is? Read this book, and you will. You may even turn into one yourself."
> — Ellen Sandler, co-executive producer: *Everybody Loves Raymond*; author: *The TV Writer's Workbook*

"I rarely think about why something I'm working on is funny. I'm usually just fixated on the fact that it's not funny enough. So it was interesting to look at it from such a thoughtful perspective. I started reading the book expecting to be merely amused, but what I found was a rigorous deconstruction of what makes comedy. Steve takes this ephemeral topic and reduces it to tangible terms that are both practical and illuminating. Oh, and it's funny. Which is useful when you're talking about comedy."
> — David Crane, creator and executive producer: *Friends, Episodes*

"Whether you're a performer, director, or writer, this is the best, most entertaining, and practical book I've ever read on the art, theory, and mechanics of comedy."
> — David Fury, writer and producer: *Buffy the Vampire Slayer, Lost, Fringe, Terra Nova*

For more than a decade, STEVE KAPLAN has been the industry's most sought-after expert on comedy writing and production. In addition to having taught at UCLA, NYU, Yale, and other top universities, Kaplan created the HBO Workspace, the HBO New Writers Program, and was cofounder and Artistic Director of Manhattan Punch Line Theatre. He has served as a consultant to such companies as DreamWorks, Disney, Aardman Animation, and HBO, and has worked with producers and production companies in Australia, Canada, New Zealand, London, Ireland, and Sweden.

$27.95 · 280 PAGES · ORDER #194RLS · ISBN 9781615931408

THE MYTH OF MWP

In a dark time, a light bringer came along, leading the curious and the frustrated to clarity and empowerment. It took the well-guarded secrets out of the hands of the few and made them available to all. It spread a spirit of openness and creative freedom, and built a storehouse of knowledge dedicated to the betterment of the arts.

The essence of the Michael Wiese Productions (MWP) is empowering people who have the burning desire to express themselves creatively. We help them realize their dreams by putting the tools in their hands. We demystify the sometimes secretive worlds of screenwriting, directing, acting, producing, film financing, and other media crafts.

By doing so, we hope to bring forth a realization of 'conscious media' which we define as being positively charged, emphasizing hope and affirming positive values like trust, cooperation, self-empowerment, freedom, and love. Grounded in the deep roots of myth, it aims to be healing both for those who make the art and those who encounter it. It hopes to be transformative for people, opening doors to new possibilities and pulling back veils to reveal hidden worlds.

MWP has built a storehouse of knowledge unequaled in the world, for no other publisher has so many titles on the media arts. Please visit www.mwp.com where you will find many free resources and a 25% discount on our books. Sign up and become part of the wider creative community!

Onward and upward,

Michael Wiese
Publisher/Filmmaker